A BRUISED REED
HE WILL NOT BREAK

By Gary Hamilton
With Tracey D. Lawrence

Published by Scribe Ink, Inc. Greeley, Colorado.
www.scribeink.org

Unless otherwise noted, Scripture quotations used in this book are from The Holy Bible, New International Version. © 1973, 1978, 1984, Biblica, Inc. Used by permission.

Disclaimer: Names may have been changed for privacy purposes.

Cover design: Joshua Jones.

Editing: Tara Plog

A Bruised Reed He Will Not Break

www.abruisedreedhewillnotbreak.com

ISBN: 978-1-61364-733-2

Printed in the Unites States of America

"A bruised reed he will not break, and a smoldering wick he will not snuff out. In faithfulness he will bring forth justice."
– Isaiah 42:3 (NIV).

Table of Contents

In loving memory, this book is dedicated to my wife, Kathy Hamilton. --Gary

Acknowledgments

From Gary:

To my daughter Brittany who cared for me from the age of nine and has been that very special daughter in my life. To my sons, Greg and Scotty, for their support and love through the years.

To Del and Jane Fast for their encouragement and belief in me.

To Dick and Carol Gott for their constant friendship and faithful service to inmates like me, leading weekly Bible studies and praying for so many.

To Dick and Carolyn Reida for mentoring me. I've enjoyed every mile traveling together to all the seminars.

To CBMC (Christian Business Men's Connection) for allowing me to share my testimony with others.

To my writer, Tracey, who through the Holy Spirit has put my words and testimony of Jesus Christ into chapters.

To Adolph Diaz, one of my first friends at Journey Christian Church, a mentor and a brother in Christ.

Finally, thank you, Lord Jesus Christ! Thank you for restoring this life. Thank you for having your hand on me and bringing me through the storm.

From Tracey:

A big thank you to the creative team that made this possible: Gary, thanks for your honest heart and willingness to let me go to the dark places with you so others might see the light of God. You are one tough dude! I'm so blessed to have served you. Del and Jane, thanks for your support and making this book a reality. Josh and Kevin, thanks for your creative work that will glorify God.

Thank you, Dick and Carol Gott. You inspire so many with just your presence. I know a glorious chariot awaits you when you receive your reward. This project wouldn't be the story of redemption that it is without your contribution in word and deed.

Thank you, Lt. Jim Hayward, for telling your portion of this story with eloquence and a humble spirit. I'm expectant to see what other adventures God might have for you and Gary!

Thank you, Pastor Frank and Grace Lescallette. Your work as shepherds of the flock is evident in this story.

Thank you, Ron Montgomery, for sharing your part in Gary's life with me and these readers. God's blessing upon you in these next chapters of your life—as a free man in every sense of the word.

Thank you, dear family: Noel, Jack, Mom and Dad. Once again, you are God's gift to me, who allow me to do whatever it is that I do. Your prayers through this have sustained and covered me. Let the Name of Jesus be lifted higher!

FOREWORD

A *Bruised Reed He Will Not Break* is a true story
of a life that exposes unrest, emptiness, evil, love,
forgiveness, compassion, sorrow, happiness ... and
most of all reveals the character of the awesome God
we serve.

I first heard Gary Hamilton's testimony on a Sunday morning at a cowboy church service in Boul-
der, Colorado several years ago. When Gary finished
speaking, I was in tears. He shared vulnerably about
how he hit the bottom—where there was no hope
to grab a hold of, in his own power. But God took
Gary out of the rungs of hell to a new life, through
the cleansing blood of Jesus Christ. His life continues
to make a difference in those needing hope *now*, including myself. Hope is a powerful tool in the hands
of God and something the enemy does not want us

to have. It's why I believe Gary's story needs to be told.

I had no idea that I would meet Gary again a few years after hearing his testimony. In June of 2007 my wife and I moved to Greeley, Colorado and began attending Journey Christian Church. Within a year, I was asked to consider serving as an elder. Gary and I became friends through our term as elders together; and I saw more and more of his compassion for the lost and needy. I witnessed more of his faith-walk, as he reached out daily to those hurting, whether they were in prison, hospitalized, battling addictions or in need of prayer. He knew how to lead people toward hope in the One Faithful Shepherd.

About two years ago, I learned that Gary had a portion of his story written out, and I asked him if he might share a copy of it with me. That evening I sat down and read it in one sitting. When I finished, I felt a strong conviction to call and tell him, "Gary this needs to go into print. A lot of people across this nation, including those in prison, need to read about God's redemption." That was the beginning of what God had in store for this project.

I feel so blessed to have been a part of the whole book process with Gary and Tracey, and of seeing it through to completion. I thank Gary for letting me be a part of his life for the past few years. My prayer is that as you read about one man's life, God will speak to you—that you might seek out what He wants to tell you about the relentless love of Jesus.

"'But we had to celebrate and be glad, because this brother of yours was dead and is alive again; he was lost and is found.'" – Luke 15:32, NIV

Del Fast

INTRODUCTION

Gone Fishin'

A day of fishing is like a day in paradise. To find that perfect spot on the lake where something will be conquered—a sacred space where glimpsing a patch of faithful pines lifts your head out of the boat as you anticipate the first bite. The stillness before the catch. And then the joy of release. There's nothing like it. I love to be alone in my pontoon boat and listen for God behind the morning breeze. He speaks to me so deeply just even in the water drops that form around the rim of my boat. And to think He knows exactly how many droplets are in this lake and in every ocean. He's Infinite, yet intimately with me. This is a place of worship with my Creator. But I also love to have company and hear the heavenly laughter of someone's first catch.

I believe everything that happens in a life is stewarded by the strong hand of God—even *when* you go fishing and *whom* you find in your boat. I mean, Jesus called out to His disciples to join Him from their own fishing hole. He meets you right where you are. I can honestly say with deep conviction that the people God has put in my path have proved to be sent to me when I needed to see Him better. One such friend was Carey Quarles, a man who sought me out to share his desire to live beyond himself despite his setbacks. Carey heard my story from a mutual friend and knew about the train accident that left me paralyzed. I remember when he first called me ... I wasn't in a place of wanting to give to others. Depression lingered over me days at a time. I felt stuck, merely trying to discern what God wanted to do with me in this dry season. But as Carey continued to call me, his resolve to meet me was undeniable, so finally I gave in to meet him for lunch.

Carey understood what it meant to survive. He let me know that he wasn't going to let his battle with cancer take away his ability to hunt and fish; and more than that, it wasn't going to prevent him from taking others with him into the great outdoors. His passion began to have an impact on me. Looking back, God had a very specific plan for our friendship. We both exchanged a fair amount of fishing stories and hunting tales, only to further discover how God wanted to use our weaknesses to strengthen the hearts of others. And so the *Wheelin' Sportman Event* was born in 2002.

Most people don't stop to think of the expenses a family endures taking care of their loved ones with disabilities. A day fishing usually isn't in the monthly budget for families, when the medical bills pour in on a daily basis. The goal of a day fishing was to make sure everyone had a chance to try, no matter what physical or mental challenge there might be; we wanted to provide all the equipment and take care of every logistic detail.

Looking through pictures of previous years, I often get teary-eyed. I love the excitement waiting for the first catch of the day. All of us volunteers stayed busy baiting hooks, emptying the fishing nets, and making sure no one fell in. And some participants just never leave your heart; they are the ones who touch you unexpectedly and in such a transcendent way that you know you will never be the same. I remember a young lady with a genetic disease, probably in her thirties, who came to our event. She had never been fishing in her life. As I was making my rounds, I heard a prolonged shriek and quickly wheeled myself over to make sure she was alright. From a distance I could see her short, childlike frame jumping up and down.

"Eek! Ahh! Ohh!" Her yelps of joy persisted as I came over to her, like she was telling me everything that happened before the big catch. She wasn't able to use words, but I heard her whole story from beginning to end, pure and full of testimony—one of the most beautiful fish tales I've ever heard. And I don't think I've heard a story since told with such a beautiful smile.

Another time at *Cast for Kids*, an event for the disabled held at Horsetooth Lake, I didn't know how many wheelchairs my boat would hold. I kept coming down to the dock for new passengers. Soon, I realized my boat was under water! I spent the day in joyful tears, as the excitement of the wheel-chair bound to get on never waned. The line to ride my boat kept growing. Talk about a real party barge.

So here I am, still alive, still fishing after seventeen years in a wheelchair. Things have never looked more beautiful sitting in my boat. And I love taking friends with me. If I'm honest, maybe I love fishing even more now than when I walked as a lively kid, free to go river-fishin' with my brother. Because now, whoever goes with me has to sit—just like me.

Surviving loss has a way of being the rod God uses to reel in blessings you couldn't even begin to know how to pray for. That's how I see it now, as I wait for the walleye to bite and reflect on the bountiful smiles of my friends who join me for a day of fishing each year. Without the accident, without prison, without hard-pressing trials, without coming to the end of myself, I would not know how beautiful life can be. And I don't mean surviving in itself is the beautiful part. God uses death, too, to bring glory to His name. What I mean to say is that all of us are survivors in some way, but what matters is what you do when you are resolved to really live beyond just breathing, despite the setbacks, where heaven's light comes in and takes you by surprise. To see the Kingdom of God fall around you though you are the least likely of people to behold it, *is* a miracle. It's a place where fishing becomes about serving others, expectant that God is about to fill the nets with the catch of a lifetime.

One day as Jesus was preaching on the shore of the Sea of Galilee, great crowds pressed in on him to listen to the word of God. 2 He noticed two empty boats at the water's edge, for the fishermen had left them and were washing their nets. ³ Stepping into one of the boats, Jesus asked Simon, its owner, to push it out into the water. So he sat in the boat and taught the crowds from there.

⁴ When he had finished speaking, he said to Simon, "Now go out where it is deeper, and let down your nets to catch some fish."

⁵ "Master," Simon replied, "we worked hard all last night and didn't catch a thing. But if you say so, I'll let the nets down again." ⁶ And this time their nets were so full of fish they began to tear! ⁷ A shout for help brought their partners in the other boat, and soon both boats were filled with fish and on the verge of sinking.

⁸ When Simon Peter realized what had happened, he fell to his knees before Jesus and said, "Oh, Lord, please leave me—I'm too much of a sinner to be around you." ⁹ For he was awestruck by the number of fish they had caught, as were the others with him. ¹⁰ His partners, James and John, the sons of Zebedee, were also amazed.

Jesus replied to Simon, "Don't be afraid! From now on you'll be fishing for people!"

¹¹ And as soon as they landed, they left everything and followed Jesus. — Luke 5:1-11

SECTION 1
YEARS IN BONDAGE

CHAPTER 1

FARMLAND

*"Be like the fox
who makes more tracks than necessary,
some in the wrong direction.
Practice resurrection."
— Wendell Berry*

Seasons on the Farm, 1950s-60s

From my ten-year-old farm boy perspective, life seemed uneventful. Not bad. Not necessarily good either. I mean, my curiosity led me down roads I wish I never went at times, but for the most part the farm was a safe place. I worked in the same fields where I played. I can't say I had a lot of happy memories as a child, but nothing terribly tragic happened either. My Uncle Percy and my cousins lived just a holler away if I ever needed someone to throw a ball around with me. If one of us Hamilton boys was in trouble, we all were. My folks didn't spend a lot of time unraveling our "who dun it" stories; it was much easier to clobber all of us to make sure the guilty never went unpunished.

My twin brother, Larry, and I fought like the dickens. One day, after a longer than normal spell of battling out our frustrations on one another, my dad decided he had enough.

"Okay, boys, you want to fight. Go right on ahead." With that, Dad squared us off in the living room and gave us both a set of boxing gloves.

At first Larry and I were stoked, ready to go. As we laced up, gearing up to let the punches start flying, I think we both realized Dad had bamboozled us.

I'm not sure how many rounds we went, but Dad firmly set the rules: "You can't sit down and rest until you both are down." When one fell, Dad pushed us back up and we had to keep going. Hours and hours later, we were still going, till we fell over beyond exhausted. After that, I don't think Larry and I fought much, or at least we didn't let Dad see it when we did.

Larry and I were a lot alike—mischievous, stubborn, ornery. But he went for the laughs more than I did, though it didn't take much to convince me to pull a prank, like switching our classes around, posing as one another. Confusing the teacher always proved to be good for a round of chuckles.

I'm not sure I was in touch with my soul as a boy, or even realized I had one that needed to be resurrected. I never gave God two cents worth of my thoughts. Looking back, it seems impossible to think I lived on a farm and didn't feel His presence all around me ... while kernels of corn grew into stalks before my eyes, turning into whole fields that grew way above my head. The cool grass, the big sky, the apricot summer sunsets. The miracles of life were all around me, but I didn't know I had access to Him back then. I believed this Creator God was "out there" somewhere, and maybe if He got real mad about my messing up, He'd send lightning to strike me down. But mostly I figured he didn't care much about me.

Me, my brothers, and cousins all worked the fields and there probably wasn't an inch of ground that didn't have our tracks on it. I loved to hunt, even the smallest kinds of critters. My favorite hangout on the farm was the slough bottoms where the cattails grew thick. I'd trap muskrats and hunt pheasant whenever I could. It was a big deal when my dad bought my brother Larry and me a .410 shotgun. He couldn't afford to get us both one, so we shared. He'd shoot, then I'd shoot. We made it work.

I know Dad loved us, but I don't remember having too many conversations with him one-on-one. For my dad, he endured long days and short weeks—and time flew by. Harvest to harvest. At the same time, we all experienced Dad's wrath on a regular basis. Disobeying Dad always had consequences, so when we deliberately disobeyed we knew we had to take our punishment like a man, no questions asked. With four of us Hamilton boys looking for adventure, it usually didn't take much to talk any one of us into doing something we were warned not to do. We'd get an itch to experience the thrill of some tomfoolery and no one resisted.

One hot summer day, we all decided to go to the lake. We each knew about the rusted raft made out of 55-gallon steel barrels. It laid in a heap by the bank, but Dad sternly told us to never take it out on the lake because it had holes all throughout the corroded frame. The mid-day heat got to our better judgment and we climbed aboard and pushed out into the deeps, all four us, along with a couple neighbor kids, Ronnie Blem and Fred Walker. As fast as we could, we took our cowboy boots off and stripped down to our underwear, ready for a swim. It wasn't too long before the raft started to sink right in the middle of the lake, the deepest part. We had to let everything go overboard, a boot here, a shirt there—and then us. I tried hard to hold onto my boots, knowing Mom would have a fit if she had to buy all of us boys a new pair of ropers. Somehow, by God's grace, we all made it in … without our clothes or boots. So we walked back half-naked and miserable thinking about the fierce punishment ahead, and trying to figure out whose stupid idea this was.

My folks were not churchgoers—no time for that kind of thing. They didn't talk about God either. But I think there must have been a spell where me, Larry, and David, and my cousins, Donny and Percy, were causing extra trouble around the farm and Dad must have thought, *well maybe a little religion wouldn't hurt the boys*, because out of the blue we were ordered, "You are all going to go to church." I always thought it was strange he only made us boys go, not my sisters.

For about three months, we set out on Sunday morning to the small Baptist church in Eaton. This was my first experience with any church. Some Sundays we didn't quite make it to the pew. Temptation crept in on our walks there, particularly when the July heat rolled in at 95 degrees. Often we'd end up swimming or fishing instead of making it to

Sunday School.

One Sunday when we all happened to make it there, all six of us decided to go forward to be baptized. Percy, I think, suggested every one of us do it, along with our Sunday School teacher, Mr. Galloway, who coaxed us too; perhaps it was that obvious to him that we needed salvation and the Lord's resurrection power in a hurry.

I don't have much recollection of what I thought emerging from the baptistery waters, and who knows what seeds were planted in me, but it wasn't a bad memory, and I think we all must have felt we had done something right for a change. Maybe Dad's plan was good after all. I didn't mind this church stuff much, until one Sunday when Mr. Galloway asked too much of me, "Gary, next week in class I'd like you to lead music for us." Well, no way was I up for that, so I decided right then and there I'd never come back again. And I didn't.

If I'm honest, my boyhood days weren't days I look back on with a great deal of fondness. I felt lonely, though my family surrounded me. I had a grass roots kind of existence. Inherently, I knew life had to offer something deeper, but I wasn't sure what. And ready or not, life kept moving me along. I graduated with my friends, was involved with FFA, and met a great girl in high school, Kathy—all good things. But I couldn't figure out why something didn't ever end up being as good as you'd hoped it would be. Though I had a task in front of me everyday and the biggest backyard a boy could hope for, deep down my life felt aimless and insignificant. The older I became, the more I wrestled with life's unfulfilling days. I didn't know God loved me and created me for a specific purpose. I didn't know He had the answers I longed to know or the love I needed. And so I began to search for meaning apart from God.

Little did I know His hand was sovereignly upon me even in the darkest days ahead. I had no idea what great lengths He'd go to just for me, to save me from the hands of the enemy.

CHAPTER 2

THE BARRICADE

May 10, 1987

On Mother's Day, I wanted to take Kathy out one last time. The months of my transgressions surrounded us both like a deadly curse. I knew I was going to be sentenced to prison the next day. I decided to make one last-ditch effort to show Kathy and the kids that deep inside I was still a good dad and husband. "Let me take you and the kids out for a Mother's Day brunch." My words fell flat. I knew it was a pathetic attempt to try and remedy all that I had destroyed.

She looked at me with sorrow, "No, I need to go to church, this is Sunday."

I didn't expect Kathy to come back and I had reached the bottom rung of existence. She didn't deserve this, but selfishly I couldn't live without her. I grabbed my gun not wanting to leave her with the responsibility of all the farm animals. One by one, I shot the horses and the dogs, like a maniac no one in my family recognized. I even killed my favorite hunting dog, Rusty.

Why live when you're a loser? I convinced myself. *I've messed my life up irreversibly. There is no hope.* Methodically, I walked around the farm and collected all the drugs I had stashed. Then I laid out line after line of cocaine and crystal meth and snorted each and every line. My mind and body began buzzing out-of-control as the drugs raged through me.

From there, I headed down to this drug house where I committed most of my crimes. The drugs revved me up to believe that the best way to go would be to have a shoot-out with the police. *Let them kill me; suicide by a cop would be my way out,* I thought as I grabbed two loaded pistols and two sawed-off shotguns and got in my truck. I figured the police expected some foul play from me the day before my sentencing, so I wanted a show.

I sped down the driveway, grabbed a gun and bailed out of my truck running toward the drug house. Slamming the door behind me, I barricaded myself in, locking the doors and pushing furniture up against the front door. When I turned around I saw a lady in the house with her baby. She was on drugs too, but had the presence of mind to see how dangerous I was. "Please let me out," she said with a quivering voice.

"No!" I screamed. "Now shut up!" I had to think about what I should do next. As I paced back and forth, a phone in the house started ringing. Staring at the phone, I finally grabbed the receiver after the fifth ring.

"What do you want?" I yelled.

"Gary," this is Lieutenant Hayward. "Come out and give yourself up."

"No," I barked, "I can't do that," and hung up. I blurted out to the woman holding her baby, "I've already killed a lot of animals today. It's over. I might as well kill again."

Lieutenant Hayward kept interrupting my plans in trying to carry out how to take care of the woman. He kept calling into the house. The third time he said something that caught me off guard. "Come on Gary, you owe me one."

"What are you talking about?" I said in a garbled, strung-out voice.

"Remember a couple of weeks ago when there was another warrant for your arrest? I told you I wouldn't come out and arrest you again. I said we made an agreement for you to come and turn yourself in. You never showed."

I sat on the other end of the phone in silence, trying to make sense of what he was saying. I knew Lieutenant Hayward. He had been out to my farm many times with various warrants. Unlike the other officers, he had a way of lowering my defenses. A way of making me feel calm while the others simply made me more agitated. I bashed in patrol cars just for a thrill, but with Hayward, I usually behaved myself.

While I was thinking things over, Lieutenant Hayward spoke again and he sounded almost friendly. "Come on, Gary. You owe me one. Just meet me outside and we'll talk."

For some reason, he made it all sound okay. I almost chuckled thinking how bizarre it was for him to suggest I owed him one. Still, it took a few hours of negotiation before I gave up. "Alright," I agreed. "But just *you*. Call all the other police off."

"Okay, you got it. And no guns. Neither one of us can have a gun."

In my drug stupor, I dragged the furniture away from the door and unlatched the bolt. As I stepped out to meet Lieutenant Hayward, I had never seen so many police officers in my life. They all stood with their guns pointed directly at me. Lieutenant

Hayward stood at the back of my pickup truck. In a loud and firm voice he said, "Gary, don't turn. Don't make any false moves." Stunned, I stood there desperately trying to think of a way I could get to my gun. I started to turn back to the house, but Hayward shouted, "I can't let you go back into the house."

Within seconds dozens of officers surrounded me, and one handcuffed me and led me to a patrol car.

Looking back, I know that day could have easily been my last. I know God's hand was on me. Three years later, I learned Lieutenant Hayward had ordered his officers to "green light it," if I made a bad move or had anything shiny in my hand—to quickly take me out. I also found out that the drugs may have caused me to see more officers than there really were. Hayward said he only had the backing of a few rookie cops with him, not a SWAT team. No doubt, God used Lieutenant Hayward to save my life—I wouldn't have cooperated like that with any other officer on the force. Though I was on the wrong side of the law, and Hayward on the other, we had an unexplainable connection. And it wouldn't be the last time our paths crossed providentially.

CHAPTER 3

WASTELAND

For the wages of sin is death … — the Apostle Paul

I really don't remember much of life between graduating from high school and falling into the drug culture. Of course there are good things I remember, like falling in love with Kathy, getting married to the girl who seemed out of my reach, and then having children. But through the good times, a malaise hung over me and the days melted together into a meaningless existence. It's like I was asleep at the wheel, waiting to crash. And it is true what they say. Life can push you along to places you never intended to go if you don't push back with some kind of resistance.

Even though marrying Kathy was the best thing that ever happened to me, next to God, at the time I didn't know how to hold on to the good around me.

As the Bible says, "the heart is intensely wicked," and without God leading it, even the beautiful things in a man's life get destroyed. Without even realizing it, I entered into a season of life where the emptiness I felt could no longer be suppressed or denied.

Waking Up to Darkness

Before sunrise I drove my truck out to the east fields and set up the irrigation systems for the morning. I liked to get at least a couple of hours of work in before sitting down to breakfast with Kathy and the kids, Greg, 19, Scotty 16, and Brittany, just 2 years old. This morning was no different. By 6:30 a.m., I had set the irrigation ditches, fed the livestock and bailed several acres of alfalfa.

Kathy set a plate of toast, bacon, and eggs in front of me and handed me a cup of strong coffee right as I sat down. I devoured my meal, kissed Kathy good-bye and then walked Scotty and Greg to the front of the house to catch their school bus. After seeing them off, I got on the tractor and headed back to the fields.

That afternoon, the heat really got to me. I felt the sun raging over me as I drove the tractor up and down the fields, chopping and mulching the leftover corn stalks. As usual, I skipped lunch because there was so much to do and not enough time in the day.

Typically, I was so focused; yet, today, for some reason, I had a hard time concentrating. I stopped the tractor for a minute and pulled out my handkerchief. Wiping my brow I stared out at the seemingly endless rows of fields. We had over eleven hundred acres between my dad, my brothers and me. This was my life-long dream—to farm with my dad and be successful at what I did. Just a few weeks ago we had received the most prestigious award in my district for producing the most sugar from sugar beets.

But as I sat there gazing out at the golden fields, I felt an emptiness in the middle of my being. For months this void had been gnawing at me, but for whatever reason, on this day, I couldn't stop it from seizing me. *What is wrong with me?* I wondered as I looked toward our picture-perfect farmhouse. *I have a beautiful wife, three wonderful children and all of this. I'm successful at what I do.* Yet, I couldn't shake how barren life felt. My eyes wandered up and down the perfectly maintained fields. Shaking my head, I forced myself to start the tractor engine and get my work done. Still, somewhere, in the deepest part of me, I felt alone and empty. It was just a matter of time until my pain grew in intensity and I couldn't ignore it anymore—nor could those closest to me.

Some of the emptiness lifted when a huge flatbed

truck delivered two brand new $85,000 John Deere tractors the next day. *Now this is hitting it big!* I thought to myself. As the tractors were being unloaded, I casually looked around hoping to catch the neighbors outside watching me in my glory. No farmer I knew had anywhere near the success that we had and these new shiny machines were proof of how big our farming operation had become.

For a couple of weeks, I felt like a king on his throne. Pride filled me as I drove the new toys around on our land. It wasn't long, though, before the newness waned. On task for the day, working the fields, out of nowhere that empty void crept up on me and again sucked me into blackness. I looked down at the tractor and instead of it making me feel good, I merely felt hollow.

"So what?" I shouted out loud, "Who cares about any of this?" I felt assaulted by the darkness inside of me; something was suffocating me, and I had to stop the tractor. My thoughts were out of control. Here I was, thirty-six years old with my farming dream-come-true and yet I felt unfulfilled. I didn't have anything left to dream.

"Hey Gary, are you okay?" my brother David shouted. He hopped out of his truck and walked over to me with a toolbox, while I pretended I was working on a wiring problem with the control levers.

"Sure. Fine," I said turning my body away from him.

Getting back into his truck he called over the engine in a loud voice, "Gary! There's a party tonight in town. You should come with me."

Giving him a noncommittal shrug I turned the tractor around and headed toward the unplowed fields. A few hours later when I pulled in for the night, my brother was waiting for me.

"Go take a shower. You're coming with me," David said with resolve. "You need to get out."

Numbly, I agreed. *Couldn't hurt,* I thought to myself.

Driving to the party I felt nothing. I didn't know what I wanted or needed, but this party wasn't about to fill the void in my life. When David led me into his friend's apartment I immediately noticed the drugs spread out on the coffee table. I was disgusted. "David, what are you doing?" I asked in a hushed voice.

David ignored me and greeted his friends. After a minute he looked over his shoulder and waved me toward him. With a big grin he announced, "Everyone, this is my brother." Immediately the suspicious faces surrounding me thawed into friendly smiles.

One of the partiers asked me if I'd like to do a line

of crystal meth and I abruptly declined, then hung back in the corner of the kitchen away from everyone. David, having already done a line, came over to me and laughed. "Come on, give it a try. It won't hurt you."

Staring at my brother I couldn't believe his foolishness. I had suspected nothing. How had he gotten involved with these drug dealers? What kind of life was he living outside the farm?

After standing in the kitchen for a while, I tried to relax. David and his friends were all laughing and smiling and having a great time. For a fleeting moment I envied them. I noticed all the nice stuff these people had in their posh apartment. A state-of-the-art stereo system, beautiful furniture and classy cars parked out front. The more I watched, the more I became intrigued.

As I drove home that night, I was conflicted. On one hand, I worried about my brother and his drug use. *Should I turn him into the police,* I wondered as a surge of anger hit me. On the other hand, these people fascinated me. They did seem to be more alive than I was and there was excitement in the room. For the next week I couldn't get the party or the people out of my mind. I began to listen to a persistent voice in the back of my head that told me I could live both lives—I could party with these people and still be the good ol' farm boy.

Friday night rolled around again and I found myself saying "sure" when they offered me a line. I couldn't believe how good I felt after I took the drugs. I felt energized, exhilarated, even happy. The dark void seemed to disappear as I partied with these new friends.

I started coming down from the high of my first line about two days later. Exhaustion and agitation set in. Picking up the phone I called David. "I feel terrible. I can't even function." Desperation laced my voice.

"Meet me in the east cornfield in a half hour," he said then hung up.

When I met him he gave me my next line of crystal meth, which I snorted down. As the drug filled my blood stream, I breathed a sigh of relief. Immediately I felt better.

And so the nightmare began.

My new life involved playing both roles—the successful farmer and the drug-addicted dealer. Instead of getting self worth from farming achievements, I began to get my identity from being the wealthy drug dealer. Users knew I had money and that immediately gave me clout—because money meant drugs.

Over the next months, I found myself cashing large farming checks and heading straight to the airport. I would fly first-class to California and buy cocaine and crystal meth, and then turn around and come home loaded with the stuff all my new friends wanted. It felt good.

Because I was tall and broad, people immediately assumed I was tough, too. I became known as "Rocker," a man trying to live up to this tough-guy image, and I found I liked the high-end cocaine the best, like Pink Peruvian. It had a better taste with quicker results, and you didn't have to worry about rotting your eye teeth—this was easy on your nostrils. I carried a pistol, wore a leather jacket, and threatened several people. When anyone bought drugs from me and didn't pay, I let them have it, beating them to the ground. Everyone knew better than to ever mess with me.

Every time I walked into a party all heads turned to look at me—Rocker. No one ever did that for the old Gary, the gentle farm boy. This new sense of importance made me feel alive again. I knew I needed to get the best drugs possible to please the users. When cocaine or meth get passed down they are less pure. You buy an 8-ball, 3 ½ grams. You take out the pure stuff and add baking soda—that's how dealers get drugs for free. I wanted the purest form and my dealer friends had lots of connections. On one spending spree, I cashed one corn check for $18,000 and spent it all on drugs.

As for Kathy, she didn't expect me home at night anymore. She had no idea about my double life, but I'm sure she guessed I was in some kind of trouble. Kathy had a grace about her that mystified me. Though I was an absent father and husband, her strength and resolve to love me never wavered. I knew she spent hours on her knees praying for me, hoping for change. Yet I ignored her, and her needs.

"Gary, I'm worried. Where have you been?" Kathy never pushed too far with questions, but when she'd ask my whereabouts I'd shoot off a mouth full of lies and leave the house. After several more months of erratic behavior, Kathy began to suspect drugs and her suspicions were soon confirmed. I couldn't hide the drug dealing anymore.

I heard Kathy pull up into the driveway, but I was so high on drugs I couldn't control the consequences of my lifestyle. She walked into our living room and found me—and a stranger bleeding from the mouth and nose.

I screamed at the client, "I told you not to mess with me!" Picking up a kitchen utensil, I threw it across the room at him. "I never forgive and I never forget, so don't cross me. You have one week to get the money!"

Kathy looked at the man with terror in her eyes. Then without a word, she stepped around him, walked into our bedroom and packed her clothes and grabbed the kids. I saw the tears streaming down her face. "You've turned our home into a drug house." Then, she left.

Two days later I got Kathy to come back home after I promised things would change. "Things will be different," I lied. "I swear. ... You have to believe me!" Somehow I managed to get her to trust me again, and Kathy and the kids came back home.

A few weeks later there was a knock at our front door at 10:30 at night. I knew who it was. The police. Not wanting them to get my drugs, I sprinted to the bathroom to grab a stash. I heard an officer say in a loud voice, "Gary! Give it up!" When Kathy opened the front door, several police officers grabbed her and took her outside while a group of other officers tackled me to the floor and Lieutenant Hayward held a gun to the back of my head.

I was high on drugs, so my mind was fuzzy. Outside I heard Kathy screaming with sheer hysteria in her voice, "My baby! My children are in there! Please let me get my children!"

With me still at gunpoint, the officers allowed Kathy to come back in and get the children. I looked over at Kathy as she held the baby in one arm and protectively encircled our two boys with her other arm. For a moment our eyes locked. Even through the fog of drugs, I saw and felt her despair.

"Mrs. Hamilton is this the way you want to raise your children?" intoned Lieutenant Hayward. The boys clung to Kathy, now crying in hysterics. The red flashing lights from the police cars flickered through the window as Kathy covered her mouth and let out a sob.

The police escorted Kathy and the kids out of the house away from the crime scene. She watched in disbelief as they handcuffed me and threw me into the back of a patrol car. The police officers began to search the farm using dogs to help sniff out all the drugs I had so carefully stowed.

Later that night when they locked me up in the county jail, I learned that my arrest was part of a big drug bust and there were 52 of us on grand jury indictment. All I could think about was getting out of jail and finding my next drug fix. Upon release, two days later, I ransacked every single spot where I had hidden drugs until I found a small stash of crystal meth in the barn. Clutching the vials in my hands, I felt like I struck gold and had found a rare, priceless nugget.

In the following days, the sheriff's department tried to arrest me on an outstanding warrant. Handcuffed in the back seat, I all but destroyed the door on the patrol car trying to get out. That led to more charges against me and over the next several months seventeen charges were added. All this led up to the barricade, the desperation.

Once again through sheer manipulation, I convinced Kathy to come home. But over the course of those thirteen months, I continued to plummet downward. Instead of getting my act together, I continued to buy and use drugs; I verbally and physically assaulted people, and completely disregarded the needs of my family. I led police on high-speed chases, fired my court appointed attorney and missed court dates. I was on a self-destructive ride and I didn't know how to get off. The weeks before the barricade were filled with strings of empty promises to Kathy. Soon, I had to pay. The farmland now looked, from my perspective, like nothing more than wasteland.

SECTION 2
INCARCERATED

CHAPTER 4

A STRANGE ROAD TO FREEDOM

"So if the Son sets you free, you are truly free." — *John 8:36*

In Bondage

The barricade led me to my dark reality. It was a long trip to the county jail that night. I had been arrested before, knew the routine, but this time there was no getting out. My despairing symptoms were obvious, so they placed me on suicide watch. As I checked through and put on the orange jumpsuit I thought, *The only solution to this hell on earth is suicide.* The dread of morning came and I had to face the courtroom. Still high on drugs, I stumbled in with shackles on my legs. All the officers involved were there. John Michaels, the police chief of Windsor. Lieutenant Hayward. The judge listened to the district attorney and I listened to the list of offenses. I sounded like a monster. I thought, *I'm really not that bad of a man.*

The attorneys made their statements and the judge looked at the reports in his hands, then back at me. After a long time of studying his notes, he finally spoke. "Mr. Hamilton, you will spend the next ten years of your life in the Colorado State Penitentiary." Removing his glasses he continued. "I suggest you take advantage of the programs and see if you can straighten out your life."

As I stood there before the judge only one thought ran through my mind. *Judge, you aren't even going to get thirty days out of me much less, ten years. I'll find a way to kill myself.* I knew what I had to do. I had to finish this losing streak.

Still coming off of a high, I smarted off to the court on my way out, "Hey guys, do you think we can forget this ever happened?"

It was strange to think John Michaels had been a good friend of mine in what seemed to be another life. Growing up in a small town, it's pretty hard to not know who the chief of police is. We used to go hunting together—until he found out about my drug problem. John, in my mind, was now my enemy. I had fooled so many people, but the games were over and the truth about who I had become echoed in the courtroom as my iniquities were publicly read.

As the security officers escorted me out, I stared at the rows of empty seats. Not one soul was there on my behalf. Not Kathy or the kids or my mom or dad. Not even a brother, a friend, or a cousin. No one. I was alone.

Jailbird

My weeks in the county jail droned on, far worse than any time I later spent in prison. There are no programs, job assignments, or things to occupy your mind. It's like purgatory: you wait for your final judgment and suffer through it. You just gotta' do your time. Weeks passed by and I didn't care enough to keep track of the calendar. But I knew when the 4th of July rolled around, as from my cell I heard the morning parade marching bands and the hooves of the Clydesdale horses prancing up and down the street. I climbed up on the top bunk and watched from the small rectangular window, where pigeons rested. The flags waving, children dancing to songs of freedom—how I wanted to be apart of it, to know what it felt like to be free inside.

Suicide meant freedom to me, but it wasn't an easy thing to try in my small pod area, since the single-tiered facility made it difficult to hang yourself. I decided to wait on plotting it out until I transferred from local to state prison.

But in the wait, God pursued me. I can't say I felt His presence or knew anything about His love for me. But every minute that passed, there isn't a doubt in my mind His divine strength protected me. My transfer came after three months. Each day in the county jail felt darker than the day before. I could barely breathe thinking about everything I had lost. *How could I fall this low?* I'd see Kathy's face and the children in my dreams and I never wanted to wake up. I felt crushing sorrow on my chest and didn't know how to move out of it. Sometimes a minute felt unbearable, as time seemed to slow down to only further expose the all-consuming darkness around me. Though she hadn't come to the sentencing, Kathy faithfully came to see me in prison. Separated by the glass window, it killed me to not be able to touch her hand, to just communicate by the visitor phones.

"Gary, I have always believed in you and I always will." I couldn't believe my wife had such strength and those words sounded like soothing music to me, but I couldn't fully receive them because I hated myself. Her tear-stained eyes still reflected love as she assured me, "I'll be here when you get out. Just get your head back on and straighten your life out." I had ruined her life and knew I didn't deserve Kathy's love. Greg, Scotty, and Brittany needed a stable home and I had taken that away from them. The boys were both at vulnerable ages when they needed a father around, and my actions broke the bond of trust. I didn't even know how to begin to ask for their forgiveness.

Kathy didn't need me, I reasoned. Her God was Almighty and powerful and I saw how He was her Rock. She knew how to lean on Him. Her God was holy; and I couldn't come up with one reason why God would forgive someone like me. Kathy and I went to church together, but for me it wasn't about God. I did it as an attempt to earn points with other people, and even God, so one day maybe I would be worthy to know Him like Kathy did.

My level of despair continued to rise. With time as my enemy, I felt tormented by my evil deeds and the devil kept my focus on self-loathing. At first being a dealer satisfied me in a way I had never been satisfied. The power and thrill took me places, like Los Angeles, places the farm life couldn't ever offer. The adrenaline rush of *almost* getting caught was a high in and of itself. But in the midst of the deception, I knew, every time I'd start to come down from a high, this dual life wasn't the answer.

The days crept slowly along, and I became more reflective; deep depression set in. The flashbacks and hallucinations I had endured flooded my memory, as I mostly isolated myself from others while I was in the county jail. The close calls. The bad drug trips. How did I buy into this lie? I let the bad memories feed my thought patterns. I obsessed over one particularly bad drug stint, when I stayed awake for three weeks. The hallucinations terrified me. I remembered how one night, Mike, a local small business owner, partied with me, and—like I had many times while high on cocaine—I had slid behind the wheel. We were flying over the roads and all of sudden, I stopped my truck. "Mike, do you see those haystacks in the middle of the road?" The drugs altered my reality and I lost control. My isolation in the pod provided hours of time for me to relive every terror and bad choice I made, over and over.

I relived all my sins alone in my cell. The flashbacks filled the hours making me aware of how much I had changed, how I reached this desolate place. During my months of dealing, no one recognized me anymore; my hair was wild and my gooseflesh skin had turned gray. Later in my room two big gargoyle-like faces appeared out of nowhere. They stared, then rotated around the walls, heckling at me. I kept listening to voices of deception that told me, "You are somebody when you have a bag of drugs."

Even some of my partying friends knew I'd gone too far. I built up a lucrative business, thousands of dollars made in minutes, and a lot of drugs were going in and out of Fort Collins. I liked those heads turning when I walked in the room and the more danger involved, the more close calls I experienced, the more I believed I was invincible. The deals I made in motel rooms with druggies and gunman on each side of the doorways, did make me pause. *Gary you are getting in way too deep.* Yet deal after deal, line after line of drugs, I continued to fly over the roads fueled with a spirit of destruction.

And the flashbacks continued, making it harder to hope or see the light of day at all.

Diagnostic Unit

White collar crimes, murder, rape—no matter what the offense committed, all prisoners endure the same conditions in the Diagnostic Unit (DU). Total lockdown. Because it is any prisoner's entry into prison life, it's maximum security.

Silence never happened during my time there. I'll never forget the screeching and banging echoing through the corridors. Corrective custody kept the inmates in line, so every order came from the guard's whistle. If someone assimilated into chow line who needed extra discipline, the whistle blared. Some prisoners weren't allowed to eat at their leisure. Such an inmate would take one bite, then wait for the whistle to signal the next bite. Again and again.

My locker sat at the foot of my bed to hold a few tee-shirts and shaving equipment. Number 56925 appeared on every article of clothing I had—it'd be my number for life, even after state prison. I kept to myself and took it all in. Every hour on the hour, the headcount started. One lever opened all the cells and the guards constantly had to account for new inmates coming in. You knew when a new troop of inmates arrived because the chatter elevated as men greeted each other like it was some big street reunion.

For almost four weeks, I survived the sounds of rage. Hellish, inhumane voices continued into the night hours, sounds of souls in bondage which echoed throughout the walls. In between this miserable existence, I was in and out of the cell, taking psychological profiles, giving my caseworker data about me, meeting with psychologists and enduring all the questions—feeling much like an object under a microscope. I felt subhuman, much like an animal being herded through an unfamiliar barn. Confusion and annoyance dominate the halls and chow lines. Men shouting with no ability to stop the torment. But it was here, above the evil clamor, where I heard God's voice for the first time.

When I checked into my cell at the DU, my plans for suicide seemed to be close at hand; the second tier had the perfect railing to hang from. Now I just had to wait for my chance. My caseworker knew of my suicidal disposition, so quickly she sent a Christian volunteer to my cell.

"Hello, Gary. I'm Rick Shepherd. I wanted to invite you to attend a Bible study." *The only thing I need is a way out—which is the right opportunity to jump,* I thought looking past him. He enthusiastically shared some of the programs and opportunities I could get involved in at DU, but nothing snapped me out of the dark haze. Before Rick left he said in a sincere voice, "Hey, Gary, if you want a Bible I can bring you one."

"Okay," I spoke without any emotion. As he walked down the corridor I thought to myself, *I'll never see him again. How could he possibly have any interest in a loser like me?"*

But as promised, Rick showed up the next day with a Bible. Then when he told me that there would be a rancher from my area at the Bible study, he piqued my interest. As I looked around my tiny cement cell I thought it would be good to get out—even if it meant going to Bible study. I knew the group met in what used to be the old gas chamber of the prison, Cell House 3. As you entered into the room, the capsule-like structure is what remained since it opened in 1897. The chairs, three rows deep, set up for spectators, still circled around the chamber. To think of prisoners executed in this man-made machine just two decades before my time there was eerie.

On June 22, 1934, William Cody Kelley became the first prisoner to die in Colorado's gas chamber, a man sentenced to death for the beating death of a local rancher. The last man executed in the gas chamber was Luis Jose Monge, who gave up his appeals and asked to be executed following a conviction for killing his wife and three of their ten children. After sharing a final meal with his seven surviving children, Monge went to the gas chamber on June 2, 1967. Sometimes there were leaks in the chamber and the prisoner suffered profoundly, though administrations tried to assure the public this indeed was humane.

All of us sitting around the old chamber knew we deserved death; you don't have to tell a prisoner they are a sinner—they know. We all needed hope so desperately. Rick spoke about God's love and for-giveness. I listened but with deep reservations. *How could God actually love a bunch of convicts like us?* I thought, as my eyes looked around the room at the men who gathered. We all had something in common—we needed to know that hope existed. I noted the broken windows, set high, close to the top of the ceiling. Pigeons flew in and out. Unlike the jail, where there were no open windows, I felt fresh air blow in, giving me a nibble of the free world.

Later that night I laid down on the wafer-thin mat-tress in my cell and picked up the Bible Rick gave me. I tried to read it but the lights had already been turned off and it was too dark to make out any words. I'm not sure how long I wrestled around on bunk, but I couldn't sleep. My mind raced through all Rick shared with us about the depth of God's love. I wanted to see if the Bible really said all of what he said. *How could God forgive someone like me? Why would Jesus die for sinners? What does that mean for me?* Words and scriptures that Kathy had shared with me began to seep into my thoughts. *Maybe she had been right that God loved me, too. Just maybe I could feel God's love. Maybe God could take me by the hand and give me the strength to climb out of this pit.*

Finally, I couldn't just *think* anymore. I had to *do* something. I slipped off my bed and knelt on the cement floor. I felt the weight of the stale prison air heavy upon me in my pitch-black cell. In barely a whisper I spoke, *"Lord, I want to give my life to you. Please show me if You are real. Please forgive me of my sins and make me a new person."* The Holy Spirit fell over me, that's the only way I can describe it, and for the first time in my life I felt peace fill me. I knelt there for several minutes with my eyes closed, letting this peace wash over me. I physically felt lighter— like 1,000 pounds had been lifted from my shoulders. It was this unexplainable lightening sensation. When I finally opened my eyes I looked around my cell, and the darkness had miraculously lifted. An illuminating light was softly filling the whole room, yet no light had been turned on. As I knelt there I knew without a shadow of a doubt, God's presence had broken into my world of darkness and He had just entered into my life. The gratitude that fell upon me I'll never forget—I didn't fully understand it all, but He actually made Himself real to someone like me.

I could barely sleep that night, and I immediately wanted to know everything about God. After my encounter with Him that night, I never again wrestled with the compulsion to kill myself while imprisoned. I felt hope for the first time in my life and the void which I had so intensely tried to fill with drugs was gone. Completely gone! Christ had filled it, and I felt like a new person. The drug dealer, Rocker—gone. Even the unfulfilled farm boy disappeared. For the first time I saw myself as God saw me—His child. And behind bars, I knew the road ahead would take me to freedom.

CHAPTER 5

LIFE IN PRISON

"We can find the good life only when we understand we aren't good." — Chuck Colson

After such a dramatic encounter with God, I wanted to learn all I could about the Bible. From reading Scripture, I discovered why I felt the way I did. Romans 7 made a lot of sense to me:

> *"So I find this law at work: Although I want to do good, evil is right there with me. For in my inner being I delight in God's law; but I see another law at work in me, waging war against the law of my mind and making me a prisoner of the law of sin at work within me. What a wretched man I am! Who will rescue me from this body that is subject to death? Thanks be to God, who delivers me through Jesus Christ our Lord."*

At the same time, God's Word taught me that in Christ I *was* a new man. "Therefore, if anyone is in Christ, he is a new creation; the old has gone, the new has come" (2 Corinthians 5:17). The chains of sin had weighed me down for so long; I had no idea how freedom from guilt and shame could change a person. The Scriptures came to life as I poured over His promises. Peace. Joy. Endurance. Hope. I had access to the abundant life now and the troubles of this world no longer had power to consume me. I had promises like, *I will never leave you or forsake you*, and, *Nothing can separate us from the love of God.* And this: "Come to me, all you who are weary and burdened, and I will give you rest. Take my yoke upon you and learn from me, for I am gentle and humble in heart, and you will find rest for your souls. For my yoke is easy and my burden is light" (Matthew 11:29-30). I began to look forward to getting up in the morning, to go to Bible study and learn something new about God that I didn't know. I felt the wounds in my soul closing up. God was healing me supernaturally.

When people hear my story they often ask, "Gary, what was prison like?" Well, surprisingly, prison is not that different from life on the street. There's greed, violence, darkness, corruption. The same reality exists inside prison as outside of prison—sin is real. I've had preachers tell me, "Gary, it's time you close that chapter of your life and move on." But, I struggle with that because it's my story about me and God, what He did for me.

People forget there are grandmas and grandpas in prison. And sometimes the only difference between the grandpa next door and the grandpa behind bars is one got caught and the other didn't. One felon may have been caught for shooting a mountain lion, certainly a real crime. But another is in for drugs and violence. Pastors are in prison. Teachers. Lawyers. The reasons and circumstances of how someone gets to prison cover the spectrum of life. Some have lived as victims of poverty and gang violence; others come highly educated, caught for embezzling money.

Guards conspire with inmates and break the law all the time. If an inmate wants drugs, there are ways to bring the drugs in. I remember women visitors who smuggled in balloons—deflated with drugs inside. The user swallowed the balloons whole to get high. Even the mail carrier smuggled in guns for the right price, because bribery works. The guards are controlled by the same things offered in the outside world: money, sex, acceptance. These same temptations were there right outside my cell.

God at Ordway

Prisoners are moved around all the time for good and bad behavior. But the Diagnostic Unit is where an inmate's profile is fully evaluated to determine the best facility for their particular case. After assimilating into prison life, completing all the tests, and showing cooperation as an inmate desiring reform, my case worker sent me to Ordway. Compared to the Diagnostic Unit, moving to Ordway felt like the good life. The mammoth-sized property looked more like an old college campus with a landscaped lawn trimmed with colorful vegetation. No former gas chamber to taunt you like at the DU, or gallows out in the yard to remind you of morbid executions. To see a lawn trimmed with flowers was not something I expected at all. Johnny-jump-ups blooming over the grounds of a prison felt like a miracle to me. Prisoners had access to a state of the art library and a well kept baseball field.

There are a lot of things that don't make sense about prison. Like chefs who are serving time and end up mopping floors instead of cooking. But somehow, I actually got a break. They needed someone to drive a tractor for the farm nearby and work the fields; despite the system, somehow, I actually worked where my life experience mattered. When my case worker called me for the job, I couldn't believe it. I made fourteen cents an hour—the highest pay you could earn.

Six days a week, I'd get on my tractor and head to the farm. Each night I'd lock it down in the shop garage. I worked the cornfields as much as I could. I didn't want to be sitting idle in my cell, watching TV. This helped give me purpose and a way to contribute to the farmer I worked for.

Being the only worker outside the prison fences, I had a guard follow me everyday. Finally, he asked me, "Gary, this is getting very boring following you to the farm everyday …. Are you gonna run or can I just leave you alone?" Both of us knew I wasn't going to try to escape. At the same time, there weren't any other jobs off-site like mine so inmates tried to get me to smuggle stuff for them. "If you go by the road along the irrigation ditch, there's a can of corn …." There were always scenarios like that, where family and friends of prisoners would plant drugs. But, that lifestyle wasn't for me anymore. I kept my focus and worked from sunrise to sunset, mulching, planting, cleaning ditches, plowing—the work was endless. My farm boss, Jim Heston, and I got along well and that would prove to work in my favor later on when I transferred to Four Mile Correctional Center. The huge farm required a lot of work, so my background served the needs of the prison in a very practical way. Knowing that, gave me a satisfaction I didn't feel on my own farm. For the first time in my life, I felt the joy of serving others. To think joy can be found in prison, well, it's just too wild for most to consider.

Ordway had a hobby shop where inmates learned to work with leather and metals. I have to say, I remember some of the men discovering they had a talent. I took to the leather work and made wallets, purses, and spent a good amount of time on a pair of chaps for my brother-in-law. On the flip side, inmates bribed the guards to bring them booze, pizza, drugs—whatever they wanted—in exchange for a piece of furniture they made. So, as it is inside and outside of prison, anything good can also be abused.

Though I spent very little time in my cell, I did struggle with the cold, bare walls. I didn't ever ask Kathy for much, because I knew the family had a tremendous burden to carry since I wasn't there. I didn't ask for a TV or a radio for my cell. But at Christmastime, Kathy sent me a set of bath towels with geese on them. Everything had to be opened by the mail room and visitors couldn't bring gifts during visitations. I'd never been so proud of any present and hung them up right away. I had plenty of enemies who were jealous of my freedom on the farm so I knew the towels were noticed by inmates walking by. You could count on the inmates to try and steal anything you had; but, I guarded those towels and no one was going to take them from me.

There were lockdowns, yard fights, and loads of trouble to avoid at Ordway. The best way to survive a prison sentence is to take it one day at a time. A fight could happen at a moment's notice in the chow line, and it could be over something as insignificant as one inmate's portion of pinto beans being bigger than the person in front of them. Pretty soon, a tray flies and the guards have to come break it up. I never understood why someone would even bother fighting over a Brussel sprout that had been boiled to death or scorched pinto beans. But it happened all the time. Sometimes I'd hear a rumor from one inmate, telling me to go to the weight pile at a certain time. That's where most fights took place and where most of the guards worked. In prison, it was usually a concrete slab, with work-out equipment, so another term for a gym.

We had a regular gym at Ordway—weights, exercise bikes, tread mills. Most of us were allowed to go for thirty-five minutes at a time, in shifts according to our cell house. But the weights were good weapons, too, and you had to watch your back all the time.

The buzz started one day, as it can. A big black man I called "Blue" said to me, "Big Sir, there is going to be a happening at 1:00. Make yourself present but then leave. Retreat to your cell so nothing happens," he warned, as he flipped his blue beads with a turn of his head. That day, he went out of his way to look out for me, and I knew it. You didn't want to appear against the "cause" at hand and not appear supportive of an organized revolt, or you might get killed by an inmate. Blue, though caught for leading a prostitution ring and other run-ins with the law, had a good side to him; he served as a barber to the other inmates and I liked him, but never did I want to cross him.

As I rushed from the gym to my cell, officers moved on top of the roof with guns—they were ready for the riot. Terror hit me as I saw rifles and the guards surround the upper tier. I scurried as quickly as I could to my cell. Twelve men instigated the riot and were put on lock-down. Usually a riot started from either a revolt against the food, mail privileges, or even something as trivial is laundry. The reason may seem insignificant, but you didn't want to be on the bad side of anyone.

I remember talking some with Troy Burrell, a

prisoner who preferred solitary confinement. Most thought of him as strange. Troy sexually molested his step-daughter. I'd watch him puff, puff away on his cigarettes and he'd always run out. Being a chain smoker, I'd hear him make deals, "Hey if you loan me a pack, I'll pay you back two." Indebted beyond what he could repay, he finally just checked himself into solitary confinement to avoid getting beat up. If you proved to be in danger, you could request it.

I noticed that the men who had a wife or a family fared better in prison. The power of someone believing in you can make all the difference. Some men at Ordway served time for years and years without any visits from family. No visits. No letters. No one praying for them. So for many inmates, prison was home—three meals a day, clean bedding, friends, and three sets of clothes. One inmate confessed to me, "For five years, Big Sir, I slept under a bridge. Most the time, there wasn't a next meal." In order to extend his sentence, this inmate acted like he was going to stab a guy; they ended up giving him four more years. For some prison isn't so bad.

Finding justice in a fallen world isn't easy. One man might be caught with an 8-ball of drugs and another guy is caught with the same amount. But if the first man has a record and already served time for it, the truth is he'll get the harsher sentence. So if a man gets five years, then he gets out and is clean for five years but caught again later, the judge will bring up his first offense as well.

Though I saw injustices all around me, the work God gave me at Ordway sustained me through some tough times of loneliness and doubt. I know it kept me from giving into temptation. When I wasn't on my tractor, the rest of the time I spent with the chaplain, Jim Whitsend. He prayed with me and I helped out preparing bulletins and any office work that needed to be done.

On the other hand, I saw so many inmates who had too much idle time and suffered for it. When boredom sets in, you are more aware of the unbalanced scales, and it is harder to hope, to see progress in your life. No direction and no self worth can debilitate a criminal faster than anything. Just like a well-designed John Deere—its design makes it geared toward specific work. If it's not used, the tractor will corrode. The same is true for a man; when we aren't challenged and put to a task our thoughts become stagnant and corrupt. We all need purpose and to see reward from our labor, because we were born to fulfill a specific purpose.

It's possible to find what God designed you to

do—even in prison. Chuck Colson, founder of *Prison Fellowship* and Nixon's hatchet man has said many times, "Prison was the best thing that ever happened to me." It's true, because of the darkness, because of the depraved heart, when God's light shows up, you are much more able to notice it. And the very sin that tried to consume you can become the very thing God uses to show His glory in the next season of your life.

I'm a believer in God's providence. For most of my years, I lived believing the things that happened to me came by my own design. I wasn't one to seek out advice or slow down too much. Mostly, I did what I wanted to do. But now, as I look back, I see the relationships in my life that were divinely orchestrated.

Like Lieutenant Hayward, who for some reason, I listened to the day of the barricade. Rick Shepherd's follow through made it possible for me to read my Bible the night I surrendered my life to the LORD. And then Mr. Heston and Chaplain Whitsend, the farmer and the pastor who gave me fulfilling work at Ordway. God put so many people in my path to help point me in the right direction. And, though I was unsure at the time, Four Mile proved no different. Providence led me with its silver cord to my next assignment.

CHAPTER 6

DIVINE OPPORTUNITIES

"So be careful how you live. Don't live like fools, but like those who are wise. Make the most of every opportunity in these evil days." — Ephesians 5:15-16, NLT

God at Four Mile

There are some people you meet in life and you see the hand of God at work, no doubt, as to why they came into your life for a certain season. And then there are the few, the ones who bless you beyond what you ever deserved. Who leave you humbled before God, and baffled, saying, "Why me, God? Why did you choose me to know them? They changed my life!" I have those kind of people in my life and it is not only one of the greatest mysteries and proof of His providence, but it shows vividly that God's grace is real.

As I began to grow in my faith, I began to view people differently, like it wasn't about happenstance anymore; rather, God was leading, guiding my path through every moment. In the past, I think most people in my life felt an energy from me that led them to believe they were an obstacle in my path. They were in my way. No doubt, I was my own man, and my way is what mattered most to me. But after surviving the barricade and months in prison, and then God making Himself real to me, I no longer dismissed His strong leading arm. My whole perspective changed and I tried to be quick to pray, "Lord, show me what you want me to do, and who is to be in my path today." I learned, too, in prison (as in life outside of it) God uses both friends and enemies alike to bring about His will.

Meeting Dick and Carol Gott was one of those outpourings of grace God generously gave me. Dick and Carol Gott were the leaders of the weekly Bible study at Four Mile. They were there for one reason: they answered the call to serve.

According to Dick and Carol, they began to feel a pull from the Holy Spirit around 1982, a sense of a calling about what they were to do. Economic conditions for Climax Mine in Leadville, Colorado caused a huge layoff of 3,000 people. Dick and two other men were in charge at the time. Though Dick couldn't see himself there for the long haul, he did find the security of the position tempting him to stay indefinitely.

By February of 1983, Dick's work had become so routine, depression set in. As he toured the plant and made his daily rounds, the drudgery of it felt all-consuming. Every day the Wall Street Journal regularly came in, hand-delivered by Dick's assistant. Dick then checked the daily market rates for "moly," a product used in steel, along with noting trends in the mining industry and financial markets; then, he phoned them in to the Western office in Golden. But one day, it didn't show up.

"Where's my Wall Street?" Dick asked, hands scrambling through the morning mail.

"I don't know, Dick, maybe they cancelled your subscription."

Dick went back in his office ... and broke down. He knew God had something else for him. Marching into his boss' office he announced, "If that early retirement is still available, I'll take it!" When Dick tells his story, he adds with a smile, "The next day my Wall Street Journal showed up."

Officially retired, Dick and Carol found themselves ready to see what God wanted to do in their lives.

Evangelista Isidora, a visiting missionary from the Philippines, began to spend time with Dick through their church in Buena Vista. "Dick, you have to begin to disciple men."

"No, Sid, I don't even know what that means," Dick retorted.

"Well, Dick, then, I'm going to pray for you."

Dick explained to me Sid's anointed demeanor. Barely five-feet tall, he was a mighty man of God. His skin sort of glowed with God's glory and the man knew how to pray. Sid spent a lot of time with God and he had story after story of those in the Philippines delivered miraculously from demon possession.

Within thirty days, Isidora's prayers were answered and Dick and Carol volunteered with *Prison Fellowship* and were asked to start a Bible study at Buena Vista.

"Honey, how can we start a Bible study, when we don't even know our Bible?" Carol candidly reminded Dick. Through this time of following God's lead and a willingness to learn, they both knew they were just clay pots for God to shape and pound out for His purposes. I love how God led them to Four Mile—they were available and God took them up on their offer to serve those in prison.

It might sound strange, but the men in prison, when they decide to commit, are more faithful to showing up at Bible study than many in your local church. It becomes like an addiction. Prison gives men the luxury of time to pray and study the Word unlike any other. Some of the inmates knew Scripture inside and out and studied the text in Hebrew and Greek.

Well, it was an interesting bunch in our study. I was in with some well-seasoned criminals. There was "Ratty" Mora, a cool kinda guy; he played jazz music, and was known for being slick. He had a way of building up your trust only to turn around and rat on you, and he'd take a bribe before you could turn your head around. But then, when he became completely sold out to Jesus Christ, his name changed from Ratty to "Raddy," meaning "radical"—a radical Christian. Raddy knew exactly what the resurrection power of Jesus Christ could do.

Then there was John Gerald, a sophisticated kind of man, one of the smartest people I've ever met, convicted for embezzlement. Before prison, he worked for a bank shuffling money around. He told me he figured out a way to transfer $15,000 at a time and not get caught. John beat the system for a while and would transfer and retransfer funds, stealing the bank's money without a lot of effort. Well, then he met a girl and took a bigger risk—transferring $25,000 to buy her a pickup. That daring attempt caught up with him and he was tracked. John's initial sentence was for ten years; upon his liberation, he married a woman with four kids. He went back to corporate America, but his giftedness became his weakness once again—he embezzled $2.5 million. Definitely, while he was imprisoned, John was addicted to Bible study.

And then there was me. An out-of-place farmboy. Home-spun, not smooth like Raddy or sophisticated like John. And Raddy and John, they'd really get into the Bible discussions. These men knew their Bible, and their questions and vetting of the Word inspired me; I couldn't wait for 2 p.m. Wednesday to roll around.

We met in a heap of a trailer that had some rickety tables we used and put together for about a half dozen of us. The flies swarmed around us because of the nearby dairy farm. All of us were armed with a wet paper towel, and we'd smack the flies and watch them fall down around the cracks of the tables. And Carol, a poised, gracious lady, sat there among the flies with us.

Everyone knew more about the Bible than I did, so I mostly sat there, just soaking it all in. If you want to hear honesty at a Bible study, along with straight-forward questions about God, attend a study in prison. The men don't hold back their problems with God or what they think about anything. As I faithfully went from week to week, I saw changes in the group. I knew it had to do with all of us, being willing to learn. But mostly it had to do with God answering Dick and Carol's prayers for us, for their hours of service, and God's faithfulness—to passionately complete what He started in us.

One thing that is contagious is a heart of gratitude. My Christian brothers here understood the joy of spiritual freedom. To be in chains to addictions, violence, and hedonism, and then to find a compassionate God in the least likely of places, breeds an abiding gratitude that few find within church walls.

Dick and Carol talked to us a lot about God's grace and forgiveness. No matter what we were in for, we all needed that. Dick had a way of drawing out the best in us and getting us to talk about how we were really doing—he really wanted to know. I think all of us respected Carol and couldn't believe she had such a heart to want be with all of us guys. Her prayers meant everything to us. Few men had a praying wife. Some didn't have anyone praying for them until they met Dick and Carol. They are the kind of people that seem to have an extra measure of gratitude in their hearts and it overflows to the down-and-out. Dick didn't hesitate to tell us how much he learned from each of us from the discussions. I know Dick and Carol witnessed many "God moments," where the Holy Spirit spoke directly to the heart of a man.

One example of this was Mike Montgomery. Mike met the Gotts in the med line, waiting for some anti-depressants, though still heavily medicated.

"Mike, we are praying for you," Dick repeatedly assured him, though he wouldn't come to a Bible study. Dick wasn't one to give up on any inmate. And finally one night Mike did attend the study. The Spirit had led them to an intense time of prayer with the men. Mike stood up with his head raised as if He could see the Lord right there. He prayed, "Lord, you know I can no longer handle this life sentence on me." His prayer continued, just honest lamenting.

And then this slight, soft-spoken Hispanic man, Juan Hernandez spoke up with authority, "Don't you know that all your brothers in Christ have a life sentence on them? It doesn't matter if we serve him in prison or on the streets, just serve the Lord." The Spirit fell on the room with great power as the men humbled themselves before God.

I know I felt the Spirit descend many times during

worship and in a way that is absent from most churches. I believe part of the reason for that is so many men have been humbled by their mistakes— they know life can no longer be about fulfilling their carnal desires. Rather they've learned that power comes in weakness. Dick would say such moments have transformed his life.

A New Assignment

Perhaps when I moved to Four Mile I had more trust in God to continue to lead me, to provide me with opportunities to know Him better. God and I had some history together now; He'd been faithful to see me through, from the county jail, to the Diagnostic Unit, to Ordway, then Four Mile. And Four Mile wasn't anything like Ordway with flower beds, a green lawn, and newer facilities. Four Mile basically consisted of a string of old trailers—there wasn't even a fence.

I transferred for good behavior, and my farm boss at Ordway, Mr. Jim Heston, had a brother who happened to be a dairy farmer near the prison grounds. Well, Four Mile, at about fifty miles away, wasn't too far, and because I had worked for Jim he recommended me to his brother, Marv. The change of facility made me anxious to learn my new routine at the dairy farm, and I held on to a strong knowing this was all God's networking. In the process, I did make some enemies because of the perks given to me. I had my own tractor to drive and a freedom in prison that other inmates didn't have. But I knew I'd be foolish if I ever took this favor for granted.

As I became more familiar with God's Word and confident in my relationship with God, I began to share my faith with other prisoners whenever I got the opportunity. I worked hard and long days, so I tried to be disciplined to use those seemingly insignificant moments; times in the barn with other workers, or the brief moments passing through the chow line, were when I could share something God did for me that day.

As the months passed at Four Mile, I discerned a strong sense of His divine hand on me. A day came, a little more than two years after I had become a Christian, when I heard an announcement over the loud speaker system: "Gary Hamilton, go meet with your casework in his office." I had no idea why this was happening, but I got up from my cell bunk and headed to my caseworker's office.

George smiled from his office chair when he saw me. "Have a seat, Gary."

"What's going on? Why are you smiling?"

"You're not going to believe this," he said, picking up a letter from the desk. "I received a motion in the mail today for a reconsideration of your sentencing. " As he spoke, he pushed the letter across the desk.

Staring at the letter I asked, "What exactly does this mean?" This seemed impossible, knowing I'd only served sixteen months of my ten-year sentence.

"The judge will read reports on you and your progress toward rehabilitation and he'll reconsider whether the time you have spent in prison is sufficient or not."

"You mean to tell me I could get out early?" My mouth turned dry and my heart fluttered as I waited for a response.

"That's right," he said. "But don't count on it; it almost never happens. He clicked a pen on top of his desk and kept talking. "We just need to get reports from people who know you and believe, like I do, that you are a rehabilitated man. If we can get all the paperwork together quickly, we may be able to get you in front of the judge in the next couple of months."

I practically floated back to my cell. I had mentally prepared myself for eight more years in prison and, now, all of a sudden, was the very real prospect that I might be going home soon. *Oh Lord, I yearn to be back home with my family; to treat them and care for them the way You have always intended me to.* I prayed fervently for the next several weeks, knowing God had done this for me.

When I stood in front of the judge several months later, my heart leaped as he spoke my name. "Mr. Hamilton, I have read all these reports," he said as he patted a stack of papers with his hand. "And like these people I believe in you. I have made a choice to give you a second chance." Then looking straight into my eyes he said, "I ask that you don't disappoint me."

"I won't, sir," I nodded, as joy welled up inside me.

"I am reducing your ten-year sentence to twenty months served with a six-year probation period."

The paperwork for me to process out of prison began immediately. I didn't know who filed the recommendation, how this all started. But, I was elated. A few hours later, while I was filling out a long release form, an officer from the sheriff's department came to me with news from the Department of Corrections.

"Gary, there has been a set back."

"What do you mean?" I said setting my pen down.

"Remember how the judge originally sentenced you to ten years, but then a few months later two more years were added to your sentence for your sawed-off shotgun possession?"

"Yeah." A sick feeling began to rise up in me.

"Well, in the hearing that just took place the judge did not include those two years and ...." He looked down.

"What?"

"You still have to serve the remainder of the two years, so you can't be released now."

Already in my street clothes, I couldn't believe it. I sat there unable to speak as a whole gamut of emotions rumbled through me. Without a word, I let him lead me back to the holding cell where I had to stay until they transported me back to prison.

Sitting on my bunk I let God have an earful. *Why would you do this? Why would you give me such favor and then take it away? God, I'm so ready to go home.* An anger welled up inside of me that I hadn't felt in a long time. I began to question God's love for me and the cruelty of the day. The divine opportunities and the transfer to Four Mile that I gave thanks to God for that morning, were forgotten; thankfulness was replaced with resentment. Anger gripped me as I let go of those grace-filled hours where I almost tasted freedom.

CHAPTER 7

UNFINISHED WORK

"For we are God's masterpiece. He has created us anew in Christ Jesus, so we can do the good things he planned for us long ago." — Ephesians 2:10, NLT

The pit I fell in tried to consume me for two days. God seemed distant and cold. I felt betrayed and confused. I kept telling God, *if this is where hope gets me, it hurts too much to dare to hope.* But then in the middle of my misery, I heard a still soft voice speak to my heart, "Gary, your work isn't finished here yet." Again and again I heard the message whispered to my heart. "Okay God," I relented. "Okay." Although I still felt confused, I had a peace—a peace that came when I chose to trust Him again. Though the pending two years felt, on the surface, like a cruel judge controlled the time I served, deep down at my core, I knew God's sovereignty trumped any act of man.

Four Mile's setup wasn't policed like a typical prison. Hard to believe that hard-core criminals were managed in portable trailers. The guards rigorously depended on the hourly headcount to make sure no one escaped. I began to contemplate what this transfer was all about, asking God to lead, to show me; and, steadily, God's peace began to sustain me.

As I mentioned earlier, my farm boss at Ordway had recommended me to his brother, who ran the dairy prison at Four Mile. Clearly God gave me favor with my old boss, which led to this new position at the dairy. His mercy hadn't left me; He just answered my prayers in a way beyond my wisdom. I did feel called to help this dairy farmer and work the land for the Lord. But rarely is work just about work, even in prison. God is most interested in His people and our relationships with one another. I wasn't sure what God was up to, but at least I knew the remaining two-year sentence meant feeding the cattle, milking the cows, and having work that allowed me a measure of freedom most prisoners didn't have. I continued to try to stay away from trouble and let God lead me.

After a few weeks, the prison supervisor pulled me aside and told me he wanted me to work with

Ron Montgomery, also known as "Hoghead," an infamous prisoner who was in for killing a state patrol officer. His nickname came from his burly build, which was like a Redskin football lineman, and the amount of time he spent at the weight pile.

"Gary, we are moving Ron Montgomery from maintenance to working with you on the dairy farm."

Oh great, I thought to myself. I wanted to just put my time in, do a good job, and get home with no hassles. With his reputation, a trouble-free work environment seemed very unlikely.

My first encounter with Ron made me really question why I had to work with this hot-tempered redhead. "I don't like you, Hamilton—watch your step." His 6-feet 3-inch, 300-pound frame brushed past me attempting to knock me down. Nodding I just kept working and tried my best to stay out of his way.

As a result, I spent a lot of time alone on my tractor, praying; and slowly, God softened my heart toward Hoghead. This inmate had a ruthless reputation in Four Mile and most feared him. Racial lines segregate people in prison just like anywhere, and Hoghead led the white supremacist group—he gave everyone their orders. No one in the yard could overpower him physically, and he really capitalized on that.

Most everyone knew Ron's story in prison. In 1975, Ron led a ring of drug robberies around San Diego. After making the money he wanted, he quit dealing and bought a ranch in Colorado. He thought all his worries were over and with his wad of money, he intended to retire from a life of transgressions. This was until a friend called him in desperate need of money, and pleaded for Hoghead to help just one more time.

Trying to act from the sidelines, Ron hired a driver, paying him $10,000 to haul 300 pounds of marijuana thirty miles. The driver backed out, so Ron ended up taking over the run, hot-rodding the truck from where they met. As he was making the drug delivery, it didn't feel right and he suspected a drug bust, a set up. A highway patrolman appeared from behind, flashing his lights, so Hoghead pulled over, fully aware he had been speeding. At first, Ron co-operated with the officer and gave him his ID. But soon information was flowing over the radio and the trooper knew the tags didn't match the truck. Ron stayed committed to the deed and armed himself with a screwdriver.

"Get in the back, and you won't get hurt," he bargained. The officer pulled his gun and cocked it, sticking it under Ron's ear. Refusing to back down, the struggle started and the gun fired twice, missing Ron. He ran back to the truck, but the officer caught up, his gun drawn; Ron backhanded him, grabbed the gun, and the gun went off—the bullet hit a main artery. Blood spewed from the trooper's chest. Ron hit him and he fell to the ground. In a state of panic, Ron shot the office five more times.

Then cops arrived and began to swarm over the fatal scene, where the officer sat dead against the bumper, shot six times. Ron would say it was never his intent to shoot the trooper; he got in the way and in his mind had no other choice. Later, it came out that the patrolman knew nothing about the drugs. The judge sentenced him to life in prison with a second degree murder charge; first degree murder would have meant the death penalty.

Through various penitentiary transfers, Ron faced adversity from one cell to the next, starting off in maximum security. Somehow he made it through four years in the hole at Centennial where they lock you up for twenty-three hours a day. No mattress. No pillow. Just a concrete cell. Everyone knew he had murdered an officer.

Through the course of imprisonment, Ron struggled with suicidal tendencies. He assumed he'd never get out, so there really wasn't much motivation to reform. He had his share of yard fights, around twenty, and four of those were stabbings. He'd take anyone on if challenged, because he vowed no one would ever defeat him. "It's like swimming with a school of sharks. Sometimes you swim around everyone, and sometimes it's too dangerous to get in the water. You gotta' keep your back to the wall. You don't know when trouble is gonna' hit and you have to be ready to roll," he'd tell me.

After many weeks of working together, we found that we made a good team, even tolerated each other. The rhythm of work kept the days moving along, and sometimes we even carried on a conversation. But I didn't see it coming, the day God intervened and interrupted us in the middle of our task. As I waited for him to load some grain, he motioned me over towards him. Making my way towards him he blurted out in a gruff voice, "Hamilton, I noticed you're always talking to the man upstairs." He pointed up toward the sky and asked, "Why?"

Stopping in my tracks, I looked at Hoghead before answering. I could tell he was serious. Cautiously, I spoke. "Man this whole thing is a nightmare," I said as I looked out toward the cell blocks. "And I can't get through this on my own. I have to rely on God's strength to help me each and every minute of the day."

Hoghead dropped his head and fell to his knees in silence. Then after what seemed like a long time, he looked at me with tears pouring down his cheeks. "Would you pray for me?" he asked in a voice raw with emotion.

In the middle of the stinky feed yard I prayed with Hoghead, that he would give himself over to the only One who could make sense out of his life, the only One who could provide peace and hope—Jesus Christ. I knew a guy like Ron didn't trust easily, always walking with his back against the wall. And then he knew people would question his conversion, just as he questioned mine. Many in prison "find Jesus," but most don't stick with their commitment, so onlookers just think all Christians are hypocrites. When we first met, Ron thought of me as a Bible-thumper—just another one who *claimed* to have found God. Somehow, that changed, and the Lord broke him that day. In that moment, I saw the same loving arm that God extended to me reach Ron, who now was my brother in Christ.

As I fell into my bunk that night, I felt God nod his head at me and softly say, "See, I told you your work here wasn't finished."

Ron and I shared a lot about God during my

remaining time in prison. Every opportunity we had, we'd talk about Him, how hard it can be to pray, and the tough passages in Scripture that seemed impossible to actually live out. Like, *"forgiving someone seventy times seven"* or "love your enemies."

I didn't know if I'd ever live to see it, but Ron's release from prison came in December 2010. I think it took Ron by surprise, too. Thirty-five years. And really when you've been in that long, you lose the only family you've ever known. It's hard to transition into society, even though everything within you longs for that day. To stay out of trouble, Ron says he's careful not to go anywhere after dark. He's proud of his '77 El Camino that has a Corvette engine. Ron confesses, too, "I still watch my back.... Still struggle with taking kindness for weakness, Gary." All of us have a struggle to face with God's help. For Ron, turning the other cheek is a tough one; it goes against everything he learned as a survivor.

I'm now grateful to God that He intervened and gave me three more months at Four Mile. And in those last weeks, God reminded me of His command that was clearly for me: *"Remember those in prison, as if you were there yourself...."* His timing is never too late; I know my sentence, right down to the minute, was the length God wanted it to be.

And in His time we find the work we were destined to do: to love His people.

SECTION 3
FREEDOM

CHAPTER 8

ANOTHER CHANCE

"But the father said to his servants, 'Quick! Bring the best robe and put it on him. Put a ring on his finger and sandals on his feet. Bring the fattened calf and kill it. Let's have a feast and celebrate. For this son of mine was dead and is alive again; he was lost and is found.' So they began to celebrate."
— Luke 15:22-25

Grace. God's Grace. I'm certain I wouldn't still be alive without it. It didn't take me long to observe that the inmates who had a higher success rate in prison had family praying for them, who came to see them, who remained faithful to them, no matter what crime they committed. I know that is why I did so well. I didn't know much about Ron's family—he didn't talk about them—so I prayed that the right Christian men might surround him. I knew the road ahead for him would be rough, but I also knew the good God does through struggle, and there probably isn't a tougher place to be a Christian than in prison. My release date came on August 21, 1990. God had redeemed me and given me unmerited favor; and now it was time to rebuild my family and pursue the life God wanted me to live. For the first time in my life, I understood what it meant to be free. Before I could go home, part of my sentence included time in rehab, to ensure my chances of success and to give me a stronger foundation transitioning back into society. I had no intention of falling off the wagon, yet I still had to battle with my sinful tendencies. Living out my faith among family would be another step of growth for me. To be trusted again would take time. Part of me wanted to prove to the world I had completely changed; but another part of me knew my growth had to come from simply making mistakes and always falling back toward God. And when I failed Kathy or my family, His Word gave me a safe place to rest:

> " ¹ Bless the LORD, O my soul: and all that
> is within me, bless his holy name. ² Bless the
> LORD, O my soul, and forget not all his ben-
> efits: ³ Who forgiveth all thine iniquities; who
> healeth all thy diseases; ⁴ Who redeemeth thy
> life from destruction; who crowneth thee with

lovingkindness and tender mercies; ⁵ *Who sat-*
isfieth thy mouth with good things; so that thy
youth is renewed like the eagle's."
— Psalm 103:1-5, NKJV

The word *iniquities* means "premeditated sin."
Not just sin I fell into, or came across when I naively
walked away from God. No, His forgiveness was
with me, even when I *planned* to sin against God.
And to think that I didn't even have the ability to
use up God's grace—that it wasn't rationed out then
capped off once I messed up too much—was something that kept me seeking Him when I found myself
slipping. As a new believer, I still struggled with old
patterns of thinking and dealt with some of the same
demons that wanted to consume me before I gave my
life to Christ. But this time, ultimately, I knew drugs
only made a situation worse; I knew my life lived
under my rule led to destruction, so the enemy could
only torment me to a point. I knew I had the power
of the Cross to draw from.

Through the drudgery of my twenty-six-month
sentence, Kathy remained a faithful wife, beyond
what I could ask of her. I knew I had a wife who understood the power of prayer, who loved God more
than she loved me. People told me on more than
one occasion, "Kathy is an angel on earth." Because

of her relationship with Jesus Christ, she faithfully stood in the gap for me, praying me into the Kingdom. I believe God gave her the endurance to persevere in prayer because I couldn't do it for myself. I'm convinced God gave her a divine portion of strength to pray for me. I gave Kathy plenty of reasons to lose hope in our marriage and in me. Yet she had a steadfast walk with God that told her to believe in what God can do, no matter what. Because of her unconditional love for me, she saw past my countless mess-ups, my miserable failures. And she never stopped praying for God to change me, to grow me. Still, I often held on to the control of my own life. I had a long way to go in learning about God's love.

I still have the Bible she read during the time of my incarceration and can sense the depth of her prayers that mark the highlighted pages. *I will never leave you nor forsake you," (Joshua 1:5b). "Do not be terrified; do not be discouraged, for the LORD your God will be with you wherever you go" (Joshua 1:9). "A bruised reed he will not break, and a smoldering wick he will not snuff out. In faithfulness he will bring forth justice" (Isaiah 42:3). "Ask and it will be given to you; seek and you will find; knock and the door will be opened to you" (Matthew 7:7).* At the top of the page near Matthew 7:7, she wrote, *Take it one day at a time. Center your life in the Kingdom. Do not worry but put all focus on the Kingdom of God, for He will get you through this.* I'm so grateful for the promises that nourished Kathy during those dark days when I was living for myself, pushing and using drugs. She grabbed hold of these promises as her sustaining power to never give up.

The easiest thing for Kathy to do, even after my incarceration, would have been to move on with life without me. But Kathy never took the easy road. With God, she walked with a bravery that is rare. Sometimes when life gets hard, even as believers, we take our struggles to futile places that help us cope. Maybe for some it is taking emotional pain to a co-worker at the office who listens when your spouse doesn't. Or maybe you feel like you are a victim of abuse and so you drown your pain in alcohol. Well, I know the suffering in my wife's heart caused by my sin could have consumed her, but she overcame it because she chose to first take it to God. She knew He was Who He said He was—the God of the impossible.

Kathy grew up as an only child, but none of her friends knew her to be spoiled or self-centered. Loyalty marked her relationships, even as a little girl. Her mother, Eleanor, wasn't supposed to be able to have children. The doctor advised Eleanor to abort Kathy because of the dangers and risks involved. She vowed to have Kathy, even if it meant death for her, because of her faith in God. I know that faith in God was passed on to Kathy through her mother. And perhaps Eleanor's own survival story had something to do with her convictions; her survival story planted seeds in Kathy to also have strength to endure.

Between 1854 and 1929 the orphan train ran through the Midwest, transporting children from all over. This was an attempt to deal with the problem of thousands of homeless children in major cities of the United States. Over 200,000 children, newborns to teenagers, rode in cramped cattle cars, hoping to be chosen to receive a home. Some children did tricks or sang to be noticed. The townspeople checked teeth, muscle strength, and interviewed children to see if they wanted them; and sadly siblings were often separated in the selection process. When the train stopped in Schuyler, Nebraska, a young couple noticed Eleanor.

"We'll take you!" the man and woman claimed.

"Well, what about my brother?" proposed Eleanor.

"Okay, we'll take him too."

Eleanor knew as an orphan what a gift family really is in this life, how love protects and shelters children.

Her rough beginnings led to inner strength, and her conviction to protect the unborn allowed Kathy to have life. The power of a mother's faith can keep families going. And that faith I saw in Kathy from the very beginning of our relationship. She believed family could survive anything.

Transitioning

Most inmates struggle to find work when they transition back into society. When I was released, you received $50, a change of clothes, and if no one picked you up, you got a bus ticket to somewhere. Not many employers are interested in taking a chance on helping an ex-con. When a hiring manager sees you've done time in jail, most of the time the application ends up in the trash can. And without support from family or friends, it is hard to make it on your own. Upon exiting prison, you receive a prison ID card and until you get a driver's license, it serves as your credentials. The stigma and struggles of an ex-con run deep. The hurdles don't end, and without support over half end up returning to prison.

Hillside Baptist Church stood by my family through a lot of ups and downs and a supportive team was in place before I even transitioned back home. For many years, Kathy attended there without me. Upon my release, I became more committed to church. Before prison, I'd go occasionally but it wasn't for the right reasons, rather to make an appearance and be seen. Now, I felt connected because of God's grace at work in me. I had support from other Christian men and I desperately needed that. Pastor Frank surrounded our family, and I felt like he took a personal interest in my spiritual life.

Kathy prepared well for my homecoming and the church had been praying for me. She did receive plenty of advice to divorce me, but she remained steadfast in her convictions, and so I quickly found myself confronted with the faithful people who prayed me through my imprisonment. A lot of people offered support, but I also wasn't quite ready to receive all their help. God still had to break me of a deep-rooted independent streak that kept me from getting too close to people. I began to meet with Pastor Frank individually, and soon I felt ready to enter into a discipleship relationship with him. For the first time, I let another man see all of my weaknesses. All the church-going games of my past had to go, and I knew God wanted me to trust Pastor Frank, no matter how afraid I might be to be transparent. We took it a day at a time.

I landed a job on a hog farm with the help of my

cousin. A farm manager he knew lost his license due to a DUI. Well, he needed a chauffeur, so I stepped in to help. Eventually he moved to Texas so I began to manage the hogs—50,000 of them. This really proved to be a blessing and God's provision for us.

Confinement hogs are completely different from the farm hog I grew up around. We kept about a dozen sows and their baby pigs out in a pen, but that was it. These confinement hogs instinctively know they are in a hog prison surrounded by concrete. There is no way out. At about six to seven months, they are ready to slaughter and weigh in at 225 to 235 lbs; a straggler might take an extra month or so to be ready.

In contrast, confinement hogs are cannibalistic and fierce. They eat a diet of corn and soybean rations, but they will fight and turn against each other for an extra morsel of food, much like what I experienced in the prison chow line. As I managed these hogs, traveling from Wray, to Akron, to Brush, I thought a lot about the prodigal son and his journey back to his father (Luke 15:11-32). The younger son squandered all of his inheritance and found himself in a famine, so he worked as a hired hand and fed a field of pigs, longing for the pods the pigs were eating; but no one gave him anything. When he came to his senses, he realized he could be under his father's covering—shelter, good food, complete provision. Longing for his father's blessing, he returned home.

Unlike the prodigal son, the hog farm gave my family provision. Most people who read the well-known parable relate to one of the main characters: the lost son, who went off to sow his wild oats; or the eldest son, the one resentful that his father showed such mercy to the son least deserving; or the father, who felt the pain of losing a wayward son. All of us can see ourselves in each of these individuals at one point in life. Funny, but I guess I related to the hogs, in that I knew what it was like to be confined in a place that wasn't your home and to be just a number, no one in sight really caring when you might be slaughtered.

I prayed a lot for Hoghead, too, during this time and went to see him regularly during his visitation hours. Knowing, too, that odds were against me, that recidivism statistics proved seven out of ten inmates repeat their crimes, made me feel vulnerable, so in a way Hoghead grounded me during my months of transition. I didn't want to forget prison life or what it taught me. And, I wanted to show Hoghead hope was to be found on outside, too. He had lived estranged from his father. Though I knew my father, I also knew the pain of wanting a deeper relationship.

Hoghead and I had a common hurt—an orphaned spirit. I prayed for Hoghead, just as I did for myself, *"God, let me know your love as my Heavenly Father, as protector, my shepherd, the one who can speak blessings over me, and over Hoghead."*

Every man needs his Father's blessing. And often we wander from home looking for it, but we end up in the far country, flailing around in a pile of slop unsure how we got there. The good thing is the far country is never too far away from God. We can never outrun our Heavenly Father.

CHAPTER 9

BACK TO PRISON

"Remember those in prison, as if you were there yourself. Remember also those being mistreated, as if you felt their pain in your own bodies." — Hebrews 13:3, NLT

Living Free

As I began to experience more of His grace and forgiveness as a free man, more gratitude toward God followed. The more time I spent outside of prison walls, the more I realized how impacted I was by the prison volunteers who carried out Hebrews 13:3—who didn't forget those in prison. It's hard for the average person to understand the desperation that lies behind prison blocks. It runs so deep that most of the inmates are living in a defeated state of mind. The pit is bottomless without God. But, Rick Shepherd. Dick and Carol Gott. The chaplains and volunteers. They were Jesus to me. They met me right where I was and didn't expect me to be anywhere else. And more than that, they had a faith in God that He was strong enough to pull me out from where I was.

The stale, heavy air that runs through each cell can be so debilitating. So when a Christian actually enters the pod, you sit up and notice. It's that obvious. The entire atmosphere changes. Your spirit responds to the Holy Spirit in them. There is a depth of evil to deal with, but when God's light enters, it is so pure.

I owed so much of my success in prison to those who invested in me there. As I continued to pray for my friends still in prison, another opportunity came up. God gave me a gift to be able to go back into prison, to share my hope with those losing theirs.

Dick and Caroline Reida were with *Prison Fellowship*, and much like the Gott's, they committed their lives to helping inmates grab hold of God's grace. I kept in touch with Dick and Caroline after transitioning out of prison and we remained dear friends.

After my return home, I felt somewhat restless, like God wanted me to serve more directly in ministry to help inmates; but I also knew the law wouldn't allow me to go back to Ordway or Four Mile, because of security reasons. And so when Dick called, I knew my prayers had been answered.

And God opened the doors for me.

"Gary, I'm getting ready to retire and I think you should apply for my job with *Prison Fellowship*."

Taken aback, I stuttered out, "uh ... well yes, I'd be very interested, Dick. To know you have that kind of faith in me ... wow."

The transition happened quickly, and I began to tour prisons in Dick's region—from York, Nebraska's women's prison, throughout northern Colorado, all the way up to Montana. Dick introduced me to all the chaplains and wardens; this was critical, as so much success on the job hinged upon relationships. We had a lot of time to talk in the car and the miles flew by as Dick told me of all the work the Lord was doing in each facility. Real miracles.

Dick instilled in me a confidence that I needed and served as a mentor at a pivotal time in my life. I never dreamed that God might choose me to be in ministry. Kathy, of course, supported this job transition, as her heart went out to those incarcerated. No one had to convince her that sharing the Gospel with those in prison was the heartbeat of God; her passion and eagerness to succeed helped compensate for the fears I felt about handling this new life in ministry. She, too, began to volunteer and join us on trips, knowing firsthand what prayer can do in the life of a family.

We began assisting with the weekend seminars for the prisons in Dick and Reida's region. Such weekends were both exhausting and invigorating. To serve in ministry along with my wife felt like an undeserved dream.

One particular weekend we headed up to Rawlins, Wyoming to lead the weekend seminar with Dick and Caroline. As we merged onto Highway 80, suddenly, a truck side-swiped the van. We were able to pull over at a rest stop and wait for police assistance. I knew of so many in prison ministry who made a point to pray for protection and we knew prayers had safeguarded us in a big way. The warfare is real and to be expected. The one thing satan does not want prisoners to know about is the hope found in God's unending grace. So he will do what he can to ambush any efforts people make to serve prisoners. No one was hurt, praise God! The van still started up just fine, so with a few gashes in the door and some shattered windows, we continued on the journey as planned.

I began working alongside Mel Goebel, the director over my region. He, too, poured hours into me, explaining the ropes of prison ministry. Like me, Mel found God's grace within the walls of prison. In 1971, Mel was sentenced to five years of hard labor in the

Nebraska State Penitentiary for burglary charges. Passing the time with drugs and alcohol, when he could get it, prison life led to further cynicism and hopelessness, until an inmate approached Mel and witnessed to him. He accepted Christ as Lord and Savior and began his ministry right then and there, overtly practicing His faith among the other inmates. Little did he know, years later he'd be working for *Prison Fellowship* full-time.

As we toured the prisons in my region my heart carried an urgency to meet the inmates, to be the one this time to say, "Your life is valuable to God and He loves you, no matter what you've done." The chaplains and wardens know which organizations are committed and which ones are not. If you say you are going to be there, you better be there or it may forfeit your chance to come back in. So, earning their trust I knew would take time. Being an ex-con, I wanted the inmates to have the seminars they needed immediately. I had to hold back my enthusiasm and trust God for His timing to work it out. I prayed a lot for patience as we walked through all the red tape; it was all part of the process to help turn an inmate's idle time into a time to pour over the promises of God. I shadowed Mel as we toured the prisons in our region—from Colorado, to Nebraska, to

Wyoming, even up to Idaho. No matter what kind of facility or prison, the story was the same. People needed hope, hope that would enable them to look beyond their crime toward a future.

The inmates hungered to be free spiritually. Most of them didn't know what the word "redeemed" really meant. And most of us outside prison walls let the word merely slip over our tongues when we sing a praise song on Sunday. But there is such a powerful visual in the word itself. The word is actually used over 130 times in the Bible: "In [Jesus Christ] we have redemption through his blood, the forgiveness of sins, according to the riches of his grace..." (Ephesians 1:7, KJV). We don't have open slave markets anymore, but picture being a slave in chains for sale. Jesus Christ comes and purchases you and calls you His most prized possession. And now that He has paid the price in full for your life, He sets you free as a bond slave to be used for His glory. Really, it is an amazing visual, particularly for those who know what it feels like to have real handcuffs placed on their wrists and real shackles on their feet.

I love the picture of freedom that we can see in *The Message* paraphrase:

*Because of the sacrifice of the Messiah, his blood
poured out on the altar of the Cross, we're a
free people—free of penalties and punishments
chalked up by all our misdeeds. And not just
barely free, either. Abundantly free! He thought
of everything, provided for everything we could
possibly need, letting us in on the plans he took
such delight in making. He set it all out before us
in Christ, a long-range plan in which everything
would be brought together and summed up in
him, everything in deepest heaven, everything on
planet earth.* — Ephesians 1:7-10

I'll never forget Nancy in Anaconda, Wyoming.
The prison had been an old mental hospital, now
converted into a women's penitentiary. I asked the
warden if I could meet with the ladies in solitary
confinement, so the guards led me to the hallway.
The doors had skinny slots for the guards to push
their food trays through, but no way to connect or
have eye contact. I pushed back the tears thinking of
the humiliation these women had to endure. I asked
specifically to talk with Nancy because she was on
death row at only age 26 for murdering her mother and father. She told me she'd been partying and
broke out in a rage over their refusal to help take
care of her child. Drugs overcame Nancy's judgment

that night. She wasn't thinking about her child or her life; she didn't consider the tragedy of losing her family and her freedom. Somehow, through this dog-kennel-like cell, I had to communicate the love of Christ to Nancy—in the most suffocating bowels of the prison, a place where no one expects to get out alive. And it's here, as everywhere, where the *only* hope that can penetrate the sting of death is the resurrection power of Jesus Christ.

I felt the chill in her heart as I tried to engage with her through the small slot. At first, she showed no interest in our conversation. But I managed to keep talking, to ask her questions. Then I heard an impatience take over in her voice.

"Doesn't the Bible say, 'Thou shall not commit murder?' God could never love me. I murdered my father and mother," she blurted out.

"Yes, Nancy, it does say that. But the Bible also talks about forgiveness. And no one is without sin. We all need His redemption. He paid for your ransom on the Cross. People often think certain sins are greater, but in God's eyes, all sin separates us from Him. There is no one without sin." I felt the weight of her offenses bear down on her in those moments. I had to let God lead me and trust Him for the right words. *God, let her feel your presence.* Nervous and excited, my heart was pounding as I tried to tell her what the love of God had done for me. I didn't want her to die without knowing the love of Christ.

I went four more times to visit her, and Nancy did accept Jesus Christ as her Lord as Savior. I continued to follow up and requested for volunteers to visit her regularly. Months later, Nancy continued to indulge herself in the sweetness of God's Word. She experienced a huge turnaround, and that heart that at one time seemed to be miles from receiving the Good News of Jesus now was revived. The passing hours now held hope, as she read about her future with God and what that looked like, right in solitary confinement. Recalling my days of incarceration and thinking of Nancy close to losing her life, I told Dick, "I can't imagine being in prison and not knowing the Lord. I'm so grateful that one of the first people I met in prison, Rick Shepherd, gave me a Bible."

With a smile of relief, Dick answered, "I can't imagine not knowing the Lord as a man in the free world!" We laughed with grateful amazement and agreed, "Lost is lost, no matter where you are."

As long as I live, I won't forget meeting Nancy.

There are different kinds of brokenness. The world's brokenness looks like self-hatred, despair, hopelessness. But when you allow God to invade your brokenness, it means facing the truth that you are weak, but strong in weakness. It means pressed on every side but not consumed.

Prison ministry isn't for the faint-hearted. There are so many obstacles to overcome and I think it is easy to say, *is all that trouble really worth it? So many fake their conversion or relapse, why should I assume it ever really works?* But I'd just say Jesus is the Shepherd who goes after the one lost sheep, leaving the ninety-nine. One life is indeed worth it. Chaplains and wardens have a tough job and volunteers come and go. Most of the time you don't see the quick turn-around one hopes for, though God orchestrates those too. *Prison Fellowship*'s mission, like many other prison ministries, is to first facilitate an environment of *acceptance* for each inmate, and then to move toward *discipleship*.

I had to try and win favor when we went to Deer Lodge, Montana. Due to a riot in the prison, we were struggling to get cooperation with the warden and chaplain there. Anytime there is an upset within prison walls, it usually means more red tape for volunteers and programming. With hope and fear, we made our way to the state capitol in Helena on behalf of *Prison Fellowship*. Five men were killed as a result of the uprising, so Mel and I knew God needed to intervene and we needed divine favor. But I marvel looking back, thinking how we made our case and God allowed us to continue the work at Deer Lodge.

Prison Fellowship relied heavily on the body of Christ for support and so much of my work meant connecting with local pastors, making phone calls, recruiting volunteers, working with chaplains and wardens to welcome new ideas of reform. For many Christians, prison can seem like such a detached concept, so foreign, and therefore, easy to say "no" before praying about it. Sometimes it is fear that keeps us from reaching out to someone living in darkness; other times it feels too hard or demands more of a commitment than we are willing to give. But no darkness can consume believers. Isaiah 49:9 says, "I will say to the prisoners, 'Come out in freedom,' and to those in darkness, 'Come into the light.'"

My testimony often opened doors to the hearts of a congregation, so they would consider serving in prison ministry. I'll never forget Second Baptist Church, a Black congregation who had an infectious overcoming spirit—what a choir. They sang up a storm, and it was like heaven's angels all showed up that Sunday. The women danced around barefoot because they needed room and freedom to move. Their souls were alive and I felt so encouraged when it came time to share my story. One gentleman, shouted out just when I needed to hear it, "You tell it like it is, Brother!"

Having served on both sides of prison walls, I'm so grateful to say that I met volunteers who were willing to meet me where I was, despite the fear and frustration of it all, who took a chance on me. That one life was mine; I was that one lost sheep, me! It's because of that kind of love that I, too, had the strength to go back to prison.

> *I will say to the prisoners, 'Come out in freedom,' and to those in darkness, 'Come into the light.' They will be my sheep, grazing in green pastures and on hills that were previously bare. They will neither hunger nor thirst. The searing sun will not reach them anymore. For the LORD in his mercy will lead them; he will lead them beside cool waters. And I will make my mountains into level paths for them. The highways will be raised above the valleys.*
>
> — Isaiah 49:9-11

CHAPTER 10

A BRUISED REED

"A bruised reed He will not break ...." — Isaiah 42:3

October 25, 1994

The newspaper read: "A Greeley woman was killed ... husband remains in serious condition in the hospital after their pickup truck was struck by a train in south Weld County Tuesday afternoon. ... identified as Kathleen Hamilton, 46, of Greeley. She died instantly when the train struck their vehicle at 2:40 p.m. near the intersection of US 85 and Weld County Road, 2 ½ miles north of Platteville. ... The pickup was thrown 164 feet after impact, coming to rest alongside the tracks."

Every detail about the hours before the accident is etched in my memory. Pastor Frank and I spent the morning together deer hunting. He expressed interest in learning how to trap and hunt, so I figured it gave me an opportunity to spend time with him and help build our relationship. I had trust issues to work through after my release from prison, but the more I became involved at Hillside Baptist, the more accepted I felt by Pastor Frank. At sunrise, we headed east of Platteville where I had spotted a small herd of deer grazing the day before. Unfortunately we couldn't find them that morning. We split up and I heard a shot ring out—Pastor Frank had found a doe. I circled around, to see if I could figure out their tracks, where the rest of them might be, and hung my jacket on a nearby fence before gutting the carcass. I planned to circle back before we left, but we ended up not going in the same direction.

"You got one! Well, Pastor Frank, I think we should come back tomorrow morning and see if we can find out where they all went." I felt determined and when it came to hunting, I relentlessly pursued my prey. So that was the plan.

Pastor Frank and I grabbed some lunch before heading home and my faith in God felt fresh and new; I owed a lot to this pastor, looking after Kathy when I couldn't. I had watched him enough to know he was sincere and didn't pursue a relationship with me out of pity or obligation. Rather, I knew he cared about me and my family. I discerned his shepherd's heart. And I wanted to keep growing in my walk with God. I knew I needed accountability and slowly I allowed him to speak into my life, though I was still guarded due to my shame.

After returning home I shared with Kathy some about the day with Frank. "Kathy, we didn't spot those deer today like I had hoped. Let's take a ride. I want to go back and find them—oh and I left my jacket out there in the Plains, too."

We got in my red Ford pickup truck and headed toward Platteville. We came to County Road 38.5. I remember crossing over the hill, but I don't remember approaching the railroad tracks. Those few details are still vivid in my mind, but then I can't grab onto anything more. I don't remember what we talked about, but I can still remember glancing over at Kathy feeling the warmth of her soul in the truck with me.

But then nothing, just a shivering emptiness. I don't remember the train being anywhere in sight. I don't remember the train catapulting into Kathy's side of the truck. I don't remember being thrown out of the pickup or being air-lifted to North Colorado Medical Center.

It's still so dark when I try to remember.

Hanging On

Doctors swarmed around the room. "Gary, you've been in an accident. You were thrown from your pickup 184 feet from impact," divulged one of the doctors. The room seemed dark and hazy, but chaotic. I had lapsed into a coma for several days, but when I came out of it I felt intense back pain shooting through my body.

"We have pins we need to put into your back and we need to get you stabilized. Gary, you are paralyzed."

In my bewildered state, panic rushed in as I cried out, "Where's Kathy? I want to see Kathy...."

"Gary, ... she didn't make it. She died instantly upon impact." I lapsed back into a coma for a few more days still in critical condition. When I woke up, Kathy's funeral had already happened. I tried to pull myself out the confusion, the physical pain, to understand the accident. The details and reports from state troopers came in the days following, like an unending storm of hard, cruel facts that sealed my fate, Kathy's fate.

I read over some of the stoic reports in shock, sometimes numbed and sometimes terrorized. "The train was traveling at 57 mph, over the speed limit." ... "It took more than a half mile for the 36-car train to stop." ... "They didn't blow the whistle at the whistle post." ... "Kathleen was wearing a seat belt and remained inside the pickup. Troopers at the scene said a seat belt wouldn't have made any difference in the death of Kathleen Hamilton. ..." *How could God let this happen to Kathy? Why not me?* I found it hard to focus. What would a future even look like?

In a rage, I pulled out the medical tubes that were feeding me life; I wanted death. The pain felt like a load too heavy to move off of my bruised body—I couldn't even turn it over to God. But then thoughts of Brittany came flooding in around the torment. My nine-year-old daughter needed a father. I had to make it, somehow I *had* to.

God raised up Pastor Frank in these crucial days that followed to minister to my family, most of whom didn't know the Lord. He met them where they were. Having a lot of experience over the years helping families through crises, he knew the touch everyone needed and discerned what kind of support to give each family member through the trauma. Over and over as people arrived throughout the night, as they gathered in the waiting area of the hospital, he relayed the tragic news of Kathy's death. There was no other option for me other than to fully entrust him with the soul care of my family. Pastor Frank knew

Kathy the best—he was truly her pastor—while most of our family he hadn't met. But during this time my family went to him to work through the grieving. Pastor Frank's wisdom soothed the hearts of those I loved. And, though they were all strangers brought together in a time of crisis, his non judgmental calm made it easy for the family to approach him.

When I started to attend Hillside Baptist Church after my release from prison, I quickly discerned who accepted me and who did not. For a majority, I still had to prove myself because now I had a label—ex-con. There were the pat comments, "Gary, so glad you're back," yet keeping me at arm's length. And part of me really understood their skepticism, why some Hillside churchgoers were holding out to see more fruit from my walk with the Lord. John 15:5 says that if we love God, we will bear fruit. The had a right to ask for fruit. There were also those who didn't try to reach out at all, making it clear to me that my sins were too sinister to darken the doors of Hillside Baptist.

But then there were a few who wanted to come alongside me and pray for me to overcome and to share my testimony with others. They believed in me like Rick Shepherd believed in me, and like Dick and Carol Gott—when there wasn't a whole lot of tangible evidence of a changed heart. Like Pastor Frank, who showed me he genuinely accepted me—I knew he was safe to talk to. Through all my ups and downs, the calls, the words of encouragement, the prayers were always there no matter what I did or didn't do. And finally I let my pride go and allowed a voice of wisdom into my life. But that didn't happen overnight.

As my sons Greg and Scotty moved through their own grief and loss as young married men, the blow greatly impacted their young families, yet I knew Brittany needed the most help—being all alone. With limited options, the family agreed that Scotty and his wife Jeana would be guardians for Brittany until I was released. But my road to recovery held a great deal of uncertainty. No one really knew if I'd make it because of the severity of my injuries.

Surgery after surgery, I tried to take each hurdle in stride, one decision at a time, another doctor's opinion at a time, trying to trust God that ultimately He knew the plan. I wrestled a lot with God over Brittany and her future. As the weeks went by, it became obvious that Brittany needed a different living arrangement. Scotty and Jeana weren't in a position to comfort Brittany. Scotty, too, newly married, had to deal with profound loss and move through it somehow himself. It proved to be too much stress on both of them, so I knew a change for Brittany had to be made. Her grades dropped and she didn't have an outlet to work through her pain.

Brittany and Kathy had always been inseparable—hand-in-hand everywhere they went. Kathy had prayed for a little girl for years after the boys were born, and after nineteen years of marriage and perseverance in her belief in what God can do, Brittany was born. I knew God saw Brittany's broken heart and all the obstacles we had to get through. He knew I had to focus on rehabilitation so I'd be strong enough to raise my daughter. My only option seemed to be to approach Pastor Frank and his wife, Grace, for help.

"I don't know who else to ask, but Brittany is failing in school. She's experiencing a tremendous amount of stress. It isn't working with Scotty, Frank. Can you help her, take her in with you?"

Pastor Frank graciously agreed. Grace and Frank made all the difference in those hard weeks while I recovered at Craig Hospital. No one knew for sure if I'd keep making it through all the surgeries and complications but we all believed God would get us through to the next phase of decisions that we'd face. Frank and Grace gave Brittany the anchors she needed. Though Brittany had always been an excellent student she needed both time to grieve and to resume some form of normalcy. Grace's background was special education and she knew how to draw out a child's abilities and work around circumstances. Grace's love and skillful tutoring kept Brittany moving toward progress and she caught up in her school work before the end of the year. In every sense of the word, they served as parents—providing food, clothing, shelter, and the nurturing she needed. Brittany knew she had their love and they wouldn't leave her.

A Tribute to Kathy

Not being able to attend Kathy's funeral still is hard for me to think about. I never got a chance to show my respect for her publicly with my family and friends. And now, my story is part of my tribute to her. Kathy knew how to enjoy life, no matter what hardships came. Her infectious laugh and merry heart impacted all of us. I wonder where my family would be without all the seeds of faith she planted in us. All the selfless prayers said in her prayer closet. Stubborn faith. My children, my brothers, my parents, my cousins, all have benefited from Kathy's prayer life. I think that is the most valuable gift Kathy left her daughter. Brittany saw her mother rely on God in the worst of times while I was in prison, and I'm certain God used Kathy to prepare Brittany to help me. When a child sees a mom cry out to God first when crisis hits, rather than last, that example leaves them forever changed. Kathy made God real to Brittany.

As Christians, it's easy to talk a lot about God and the need to have faith, but quite another to act on it. Kathy believed in her God up to the very moment life left her body. As I share this tribute, my prayer is for all those who have given up on a loved one to ask God for strength to hang on to hope, to believe though it hurts to believe. Kathy would say, *don't ever give up.* Perhaps you are ready to walk out on your spouse and you have declared your marriage to be dead. Kathy would say, "Speak to the mountain and God will move it. Never stop loving, never stop praying."

I'm certain her prayers have carried us through the years even now. We still see the fruit from them in our own lives, as we face this season of life with its battles and victories to plow through. All those silent prayers she said for me to trust in God, to let go, I know they are still with me, strengthening me to press forward with God. And her prayers for Brittany to be a Christ-follower? I am a witness to the promise, "Train up a child in the way they should go and (s)he will not depart from it." Pastor Frank saw Kathy walk through some violent storms with me, so he knew firsthand what fueled her and what kept her going: Faith in God.

And God keeps working on all of us. I pray blessings over Greg, Scotty, and Brittany's family now—that they continue to discover how much God loves them, the very height, width, and breath of His love and that they would find great joy in serving Him all their days. I pray for each of my grandchildren by name—Kirk, Kayla, Brooke, Nathan, and Bridger. I pray that God would bless the Hamilton family for generations to come, that we might be known, against all odds, as followers of Jesus Christ.

CHAPTER 11

FOR KATHY

*Charm is deceptive, and beauty does not last; but a woman who fears the L*ORD *will be greatly praised. Reward her for all she has done. Let her deeds publicly declare her praise.*
— *Proverbs 31:30-31*

In honor of her life and memory, I share this chapter as a way to lift up Kathy's testimony, the God-seed that was planted in my family. I share the words God gave Pastor Frank all those years ago at her funeral. I disclose it as a tribute to her life and know she is cheering us on as a part of the "great cloud of witnesses." I pray it blesses all those who did not have the privilege of knowing her.

For Kathy Marie Hamilton (1948-1994)
Memorial Service, Hillside Baptist
Pastor Frank Lescallette
October 28, 1994

Tuesday afternoon of this week we were reminded again in an abrupt way of the brevity of life. During the last three days we have struggled with questions and concerns that are way beyond anything we know. As I turned to God's Word a verse came to me that I want to talk with you about. That verse is found in John 16:33.

It reads: "These things I have spoken to you, that in me you may have peace. In the world you have tribulation, but take courage, I have overcome the world."

When Jesus spoke these words He stood near the end of His life. He knew what was going to happen to these disciples and He wanted to help, to encourage and to prepare them just as He wants to help us today.

May I point out to you some of what God is saying to us today. We have been brought face to face with three realities which we need to face.

The first reality is that in the world you will have tribulations or sufferings. In the world you have tribulation. Tribulation was vivid for Jesus and His disciples. This word comes from the threshing of wheat, beating it against the ground so the tassels of grain would fall off or having an animal walk on it tearing the tassels off. This was the picture of tribulation in Jesus's mind as He spoke.

In the world we are going to have tribulation or struggles or sufferings. The world will beat us down and try to take us apart. It will attempt to take the things and people we love from us, days like last Tuesday when life brought us face-to-face with events we do not want. Events we do not want to experience and cannot control. Our Lord tried to tell us about trouble and suffering. He assured us that these would come but that we would not have to face them alone. He tried to explain and warn us but nothing could have prepared us for these events.

Kathy moved quickly from her presence here to the presence of her Lord leaving us with a giant empty place in our hearts and lives. Gary's condition continues to be stable but critical. We still don't know what the future holds for him so a part of our prayers is to plead with our Lord for insight, understanding and courage as we continue to walk with Him hour by hour, day by day.

These are events we did not want and struggle to endure. Tribulations or sufferings continue to overwhelm us. Just when we think we have a handle on our emotions and the circumstances, they change.

It is in these times of uncertainty that God wants us to remember again and again that He will not leave us alone. He will come to us. Let me remind you that He did not say He would send someone but that He would come Himself to walk with us through these events. I know you are locked into circumstances you cannot ignore and cannot escape. Sufferings of which you have never known.

John recorded Jesus's promise in John 14:18:

> *"I will not leave you comfortless, I will come to you. I will not leave you alone in the storm, I will come to you."*

Those who know Jesus as Savior can be assured that He does not send help He brings it Himself, personally. In the deepest struggle and darkest night God hears your call and will come walk with you through this valley and on to the mountain top where you will be able to see the brightness of the future and put the past into perspective.

Something like what has happened to you, happened to Jesus. A wonderful friend named Lazarus who was like family to Him died suddenly. Jesus arrived and asked his sisters where they had buried him. They took Him to the place where His friend had been placed.

As they stood there you could see the emotions

welling up within Jesus which soon burst out in tears. The shortest verse in the Bible is John 11:35 where we read: "Jesus wept," not because Lazarus had died because He knew what He could do, but He wept because He knew what it felt like to suffer the loss of someone and He knew what this family and their friends were suffering.

None of us are immune. Today we are reminded of all the push and shove, the rub and hurt of life. Jesus said you are going to have tribulation and suffering but that is not all Jesus said. He said I am speaking to you that I will supply what you need.

The second reality is that you can have peace.

Not only did He know about the realities of life but He knew about the reality that we could have peace in the midst of anything the world could throw at us if we love and follow Him. The peace that comes no matter what the circumstances. He has the words of life and hope and words about the future.

If I asked you to write a definition of peace most of us would write something like a quietness or calmness. But peace is an active kind of word which reaches out and puts life back together in the present and assures us of eternity and peace in our future.

Jesus said. I want you to know that the world tears at your lives, but He also said I have come to put your lives back together. They will never be the same but if you continue to have faith and walk with God He will walk with you here and then hereafter where we will join those who have gone on before. I have spoken this to you because I want you to have peace.

There is no doubt in my mind that the Lord is with us. I wish He had given us more answers. Gary asked me yesterday morning first thing, Why? Why? But I am like you, I don't know why because I don't know how God is using these circumstances to help you grow, mature and put your lives back together.

It does look like everything is coming apart right now. He did not cause these circumstances but he will use them to help you trust him more, to live more faithfully and ultimately to be with Kathy again—and that time will be forever.

That is what the word peace means in the Bible and in our world. To those who have faith in Him, God gives us peace with Him, peace with others and peace with things. When you have this peace in this order your lives will be full and complete again just as God intended when he breathed life into you and said live. Above everything the world can throw at us God says, "I have overcome the world." Trust me, it is done, and you will see it in the days ahead.

To illustrate this God allowed Jesus to be killed and

the world to pull and punish, hit and hurt Him and in turn His disciples, but He came to them from beyond the grave to help them understand and believe.

He stood in their midst alive beyond the grave to say ... 'Trust me and believe, I have overcome the world with all its pain and suffering. Just as I have raised myself, just as I have raised Kathy Hamilton, I will take care of you and provide a place where all those who believe will gather together and this time for eternity.'

This very day in this very difficult situation God is going to use these moments, this experience, to put something together for good in His Kingdom's work and in your lives. We will see it clearer as we move away from what we have experienced in these last days.

All things do work together for good not that all things are good. But that all things work together for good to those who love God. Somehow even in the premature analysis, He is working it out in a meaningful way that will make a difference in His Kingdom's work and in your lives in the days and years to come.

You say, Pastor, 'I don't understand that,' and I must say as I have said to Gary and to this family I don't understand it either, but I believe what God says, and I believe He can do that and I believe I have seen Him do that in the lives of others. *As He weaves your lives back together watch for Him, listen to Him and He will show you the way. Remember this life is temporary—no one gets out of this life alive but to those who have faith God, who allow Him to unite His life with our lives. We will spend eternity with Him and with all those who have gone before us who believe and are faithful. That is the perspective we must hang on to.*

One final thought. Not only does our Lord speak to us about the reality of life and the promise of peace but His Word here ends in His challenge to have courage for He has overcome the world.

The third reality is that God has already overcome the world. He speaks to us about having courage in tribulation, having courage in struggles and suffering.

Kathy had courage and strength for everyone in this family that needed it. She understood something all of us need to understand and that was that Jesus has never lost a person. She endured many struggles and sufferings and quietly kept walking in faith and trusting God.

You and I have lost a friend, a mother, a wife, a grandmother, a church member, a loved one, an in-law, but the Lord has never lost anyone. He says, have courage I have overcome everything this world can do to you.

I have even overcome death and provided a place for all those who are faithful to gather and spend eternity together. So, there is help and here is hope and there is heaven, and I am here to remind you of what Kathy would tell you from experience. Her quiet faith and courage provide us with an example of how our lives should be lived here and ultimately in Heaven.

The world will try to take you apart, but Jesus came to put your lives back together. So take courage, He has overcome the world. The world just does not know it yet. Then she would say:

*¹ The LORD is my shepherd, I lack nothing. ²
He makes me lie down in green pastures, he leads me beside quiet waters, ³ he refreshes my soul. He guides me along the right paths for his name's sake.*
⁴ Even though I walk through the darkest valley, I will fear no evil,
for you are with me; your rod and your staff, they comfort me. ⁵ You prepare a table before me in the presence of my enemies.
You anoint my head with oil; my cup overflows. ⁶ Surely your goodness and love will follow me all the days of my life, and I will dwell in the house of the LORD forever.
—— Psalm 23

When I think of Kathy Hamilton I think of a faith-ful, loving sincere wife, mother, grandmother, in-law, loved one, friend, church member, helper and teacher. One who believed in prayer. Kathy believed you could pray to the Lord for anything and He would hear. You went on with your life and as He worked it out, God would grant your prayer according to His will and His time.

Brittany is living proof of such a life of prayer. Kathy asked God for a little girl a long time before it happened. She went on with her life and when the time was right, along came Brittany.

Then there is Gary whom she has prayed for and loved through many years. This entire family has been touched and influenced by her attitude of prayer.

Maybe she has touched our lives as much as our Lord intended and that is why He has allowed her to come live with Him leaving us to follow her faithful example with the knowledge that one day when God is ready we will be able to join her.

One of her sons said of his mom. "In twenty-three years, I do not have one bad memory of Mom. She was always up, working, and going to work but ready to help with homework or whatever I needed."

Another son said: "When I think of Mom, I think of her soft smile no matter what was going on."

The Bible describes a woman like Kathy as a:
"truly good wife
worth more than precious gems.
Her husband can trust in her
and she will rightly satisfy his needs.
She will not hinder him but help him
all her life....
She gets up before dawn
to prepare breakfast for her family....
She is energetic, and a hard worker.
She provides for her children
and meets their every need....
She is a woman of strength and dignity.
Her words are wise
and kindness is the rule for everything she says....
Her children stand and bless her
and so does her husband.
He praises her with these words:
There are many fine women in the world
but you are the best of them all.
Charm can be deceitful and beauty does not last
but a woman who fears and reverences God
shall be greatly praised."
— Proverbs 31

If Kathy ever wanted you to live by faith and get on with your lives it is now. She would say, trust God, have faith, love one another, and become the family I lived and prayed for.

In the world your will have suffering—it is inevitable—but remember God has overcome the world and even the events which brought us here today. Amen!

CHAPTER 12

A SMOLDERING WICK

*" ... a smoldering wick he will not snuff out, till he leads justice
to victory." — Isaiah 42:3b, NIV*

Rehab

In the months of rehab at Craig Hospital, I focused
on getting better so I could be strong enough to take
care of Brittany. Though the mental battles far out-
weighed the physical, my therapists continued to
point out the need for me to direct my energy toward
getting better, to not worry about all the things that
tried to bog me down—medical bills, provision, Brittany's future. The boys didn't need me like Brittany
did, but I needed to be well for them, too.

As I worked through physical therapy, I attempted
to accelerate the process as much as possible, but
mentally the battles raged on, and I couldn't fight

and resolve them all at once. I lost my wife, lost my marriage of twenty-eight years, and lost the use of my legs in a matter of seconds. But clearly God wanted me to move beyond the loss and find healing in brokenness. And that is a lot right there to make me pause and remember. But He didn't expect that to happen overnight.

Visits from Pastor Frank and Brittany helped push me forward. My physical therapy sessions were tough on Brittany. I saw fear and anger in her eyes as the therapists pushed me to my limits. I had to learn to get through any life situation as a paraplegic, so she saw the coach throw the ball at me, so hard that I'd fall down. They pressed me toward the edge of defeat, but never to the point of complete despair. Somehow that reserve in me kept pushing forward and I'd maneuver around it.

"Daddy, why are they so mean, pushing you down like that?"

"Brittany, it's okay. It's making me stronger, so we can be together."

To be attached to the wheelchair, something me-chanical and foreign, went against my nature. It wasn't the controls on my wheelchair that were frustrating—I was used to farm equipment—but rather it was feeling like it now defined me. Gently and slowly, God helped me to see that the wheelchair wasn't my enemy. Joni Eareckson Tada, a quadriplegic for over forty years—one of the longest durations on record—ministered to me in my transition as I read her honest prose. She encouraged me, as I wrestled with being disabled, that disability does not have to be the end of the world. Her faith was breathtaking to me.

When gratitude finally broke through in me, everything changed, which happened after about ten weeks of rehab at Craig Hospital. Waiting for Brittany's visit at the elevator, I noticed a man paralyzed from the neck down with his three children. His wife hoisted each child up, one at a time to their Daddy's face, so he could see them and feel their cheeks on his. The elevator opened and Brittany ran towards me and jumped on my lap. I opened my arms as wide as they'd go and rejoiced that I could feel her arms hugging me back. From there, God convicted me of something—I really did have so many blessings to count through the horrors of the accident. I began to praise God for simple things: that I could feel Brittany when she sat on my lap, that I could hug her still and had use of my arms. We both watched the quadriplegic with admiration as his family all continued to hug their daddy's neck.

Joni wrote, "God uses suffering. He lobs it like a hand grenade and blows to smithereens these notions we have about our self and who we think we are. Blows it to smithereens until we are left raw, naked, and we have to let suffering do its work." In some ways, I was helpless, but in that state of mind, I let go of control and began to follow Him like never before.

As the time approached for me to be released, Pastor Frank and the church helped Brittany and me find an apartment that accommodated me and my wheelchair. When I think of His miraculous provision even now, I weep because He provided beautifully for us all along the way. With the medical bills piling up every day, I had to rely on God's resources. Our church paid for our new place, to get us going. No one who gave toward our apartment really knew if the day would ever come when I'd actually go home—but it did. And the day couldn't come soon enough for me, so much so I refused to take a class my doctors recommended: How to Recover When Your Wheelchair Turns Over. "No thanks," I said without blinking, "I have no intention of falling out of my wheelchair." And so they let me go.

Scotty came to get me that evening. When I received the formal release, I darted out those hospital doors in my chair with great conviction. I didn't get too far and wasn't prepared for the speed bump in the road—and wham! I tipped over. A saw headlights coming straight at me and I had no idea if the driver spotted me. Thankfully Scotty was trailing right behind me and the car slammed on the brakes. Scotty and some of the hospital staff took me back into Craig. Humbly, and with a smidge of disgrace, I enrolled in the class.

The apartment near Craig Hospital taught me so much about what life now looked like for me. There were times I was scared working through all the adjustments, getting to know my limits physically. Clothing myself and taking a shower weren't just quick, morning-routine tasks anymore. I had to be safe, think wisely, take my time. Some things were pushing the limits of being possible and I had to know what those things were. For any man to have to focus on what you lack can be painfully humbling. I'd wheel over to Craig each day for more tests and therapy and, as the days went by, I did develop the confidence I needed to function.

There was a tunnel from Craig to Swedish Hospital. I'd wheel through, watching people on gurneys go by heading to surgery. I can't even count how many times the gurney being wheeled off for more tests, more surgeries, happened to be me. The tunnel always seemed longer every time I'd pass through it. I knew how many lights lined the lower walls. I knew which tiles were missing. I'd count anything to occupy my mind. And then when I passed through the long-block tunnel, most of the time it meant waiting. I'd lay there and lay there. Waiting and waiting. And after so many days of it, I realized there wasn't a thing I could do about it; I wasn't going anywhere and so I had to be content to just wait. And I discovered this time with God as a gift ... God's presence with me *in* the waiting. All this dreaded time really proved to be an opportunity to be with my Heavenly Father—just me and Him.

In these weeks it also became clear that I needed to resign from *Prison Fellowship*. I put off writing the resignation letter to Mel as long as I could, but finally I knew God wanted me to let it go.

I remember asking Pastor Frank, "So strange to even say this, but why do I feel so close to God in this tragedy, when all around me is loss?" What he said made a whole lot of sense.

"Gary, it's because you are letting God carry the football. You know you can't even consider taking your eyes off of Him."

I must have gone through hundreds of tests over

the seventh-month period at Craig. Though I can't remember what this particularly intimidating test accomplished, I remember being immersed in water and put into a big barrel. Fear began to well up inside of me as I was completely helpless, like a baby. "God, I feel like a sinking ship. Please help me."

And I heard Him say to me, "Trust in Me. Trust in *Me*. I have not abandoned you. ... I sent my Son to die for you." It's when you are most broken that you hear Him the loudest.

Bonding

Before the accident, I knew Kathy and Brittany had a very special, God-given mother-daughter bond. Since I loved working for *Prison Fellowship* and immersed myself in serving the prisons assigned to me, my time away from family was unavoidable. Work took me away in the evenings and weekends as well. So in a lot of ways, Brittany and I had to get to know each other in a new way.

Hillside Baptist truly went well beyond what we ever could have asked. The church bought me my first wheelchair-accessible van and I began to drive again. We couldn't go back to our house, which had no ramp or wheelchair provisions for me, so Pastor Frank went out on a hunt and found us our first apartment.

Brittany and I started off with one very important thing in common—we both needed to know we weren't alone in all of this. She still had fear, anger, doubt, angst, and it needed a safe place to be released. And so did I. Even then, I couldn't bear to think how much pain her small heart had to endure.

I watched her teach herself how to cook. She grabbed Kathy's recipes, taking special note of the cookbooks held together with rubber bands and paper clips that looked most used, and started experimenting, making grocery lists and taking inventory of the kitchen items. I marveled at her industrious heart. She grew up helping her mom every day, so cleaning the apartment and doing the household chores came easy for her; at least she made it look easy. In between her new domestic responsibilities, she had to keep up with her school work, limiting herself to a few friends, but not wanting to commit to too many outside activities away from me. We were getting stronger in teamwork and both of us knew when we turned the first major corner—we bonded as father and daughter.

Quickly, I found myself relying on her. At times it felt like she was raising me, rather than *me* raising her. Somehow we found a groove and we were making it work. Physically, my body felt the toll of all the surgeries. When the steel rods went into my back, I laid flat for six weeks in the hospital due to the blood clots in my lungs and legs. Not being able to see outside made it feel like prison all over again. Finally I gained some strength and the nurse took me over to the window. The warm sun fell on me, but I still couldn't see out. I had thought to myself, *I'll never see the outside world again.* But here I was moving around inside my apartment, and outside of my apartment driving us around.

For the most part, we were making it, but I didn't know how to reach Brittany's emotional pain. She fought back the tears so many times to be strong for me, so I wouldn't know she was hurting. Then after a couple of years, one of Brittany's teachers called.

"Gary, she cries a lot. She's taken on a lot for her age. We recommend that you go to hospice care counseling to help Brittany grieve." I agreed to pursue counseling and thanked the teacher for the call.

The counselors exposed the dynamics that we still had to work through. Brittany had readily accepted so much responsibility, having to grow up so quickly. And in addition, I didn't verbalize the loss of Kathy. Talking with others who lost loved ones provided a place for Brittany to see healthy ways to talk about loss.

"Mr. Hamilton, Brittany has learned to verbalize her grief and she is doing much better emotionally than you. You have learned to keep it inside, but Brittany needs you to also let it out." God used this time to bring more healing for me and it also brought more healing to Brittany because she saw me deal with it in front of her with the help of the grief counseling. As I listened to other testimonies and tragedies, Brittany saw me empathize, weep, and acknowledge the real pain I felt. Our bond continued to grow.

When Brittany opened up I learned more about what she endured during the first week of the accident:

"Dad, I saw the pickup at the junkyard. We drove by on our way to the hospital. Scotty started throwing up and had to stop driving. … I heard you tell Uncle David at the hospital to turn the machines off and pull the plugs so you could just die. I hated seeing you tied down like that, ready to die. … I was so scared I'd lose you too—so scared. I don't remember the funeral much or what Pastor Frank said. But I did get to help pick the roses on Mom's casket. I'm glad I still have them. Dad, it didn't look like Mom in the casket. All her bones were crushed, and

I hated saying goodbye to her. ... But you know what God did for me? A few days after Mom died, I had a dream. Jesus came to me and I saw Him in a white robe, next to Mom. He said, 'She will be with you forever.' And later, I had another one. Mom was sitting, holding me, telling me she loved me and was with me no matter where I went. ... I keep praying for more dreams."

We wept together. I learned from Brittany to take every tear to God. And as Jesus wept with Mary and Martha when Lazarus died, I knew He was weeping with us, too.

We were coming to a close of our therapy and the instructor made a request that left me feeling unsettled. "Light this candle. This symbolizes your loved one." I lit the candle and smiled envisioning Kathy's smile. "Now, okay. It's time to say goodbye. Blow out the candle." *What?* That didn't make sense to me. I didn't get it, and with conviction decided not to do it. Kathy wasn't gone—she was forever alive with Jesus. *Why would I blow out her flame?* I proudly let it burn, watching the wick spin and glow around the smoke. I knew Kathy fulfilled her purpose on earth. The Lord had His reasons to take her when He did. And I thanked God for giving her eternal life. No tragedy, no demon, no circumstance, could snuff out her life with God. And I knew the same was true for me.

Brittany and I kept going to church. We knew we needed support to survive. I knew if I neglected fellowship with other believers I'd wither up in my own pool of bitterness, anger, and isolation. I also knew Brittany needed to hear God's Word as much as possible, so I could continue what Kathy had started, teaching Brittany to walk with God through everyday life.

The hardest thing about being a parent was figuring out if I handled things right. Brittany didn't give me problems, instead we both were dealing with our own battles *inside*. I prayed a lot for balance, that I'd depend on Brittany the way God wanted me to, but also trust God to show us the things that each of us had to overcome with God alone. Sometimes the obstacles that surrounded us seemed to block out any hope of getting around them all. And unexpectedly, my wheelchair started to become the very thing that kept me connected with God, so that I had to stay in constant communication with Him, and listen to His counsel. And I knew His counsel also came through the means of other godly men.

"Pastor Frank. I received the train accident settlement money. If I just take this money into my own hands, I know I'll blow it. Brittany's future is at stake, too. Can you help me steward this properly?" And as always, Pastor Frank came through. He introduced me to a president of a local bank and I met some financial advisors. I knew God still had the football in His hand and I just needed to watch Him work. The old Gary would have said, "I don't need anyone to tell me what to do." But I finally began to see how God was using my brokenness. I had to accept this discipline of suffering, His cleansing fire, where He was emptying me of "self." And in that process, I learned to lean on the godly people that He placed in my path, entrusting them with my life and even the lives of my family.

CHAPTER 13

FRIENDS FROM HIGH PLACES

"The mind of man plans his way, But the LORD directs his steps." — Proverbs 16:9

Retrospect

Looking back through the years, I can only conclude that I've had friends from high places step into my path, even when I willfully chose the wrong place. My wife, Kathy. Lieutenant Jim Hayward. Marv, my farm boss at Ordway. Hoghead. Dick and Carol Gott. Mel Goebel at *Prison Fellowship*. Dick and Caroline Reida. There are so many more, but I'm humbled to think of what each person has taught me, and how I might have gone another direction without knowing them.

On the day of the barricade, if Lieutenant Hayward hadn't been on duty at that time of day, I may not be alive. *What if my arrest had been scheduled on his day off?* I had no intention of backing down from my state of rebellion and planned for my suicide. All the other officers I knew set me off and brought out the worst in me. But when Jim showed up to that farmhouse, I cooperated—he brought out my conscience. To think years later, I'd have the privilege of serving on the board for Christian Businessman's Committee with him, to be on the same team working to support a ministry, isn't something I ever imagined was possible. I don't think many ex-cons expect to become close friends with their arresting officer.

God used him strategically on the day of the barricade, but also in the length of my prison sentence. When I first received news from my case worker about my reduced sentence, that joyful and too-soon-terrible day, Jim actually had a lot to do with why the orders came back for me to serve three more months. God used him in such a strategic way that day. He reminded the judge of the sawed-off shotgun in my possession the day of the arrest. That alone was a twenty-four month sentence, so the judge made sure I did at least that. When reviewing my case, they forgot about the unconcealed weapon in the back of my truck. Jim called that violation to attention, so the judge added three more months.

But in those agonizing months, I met Hoghead, and Hoghead met the Lord. God's control proved to be at work in much more powerful ways that I understood at the time.

Hoghead did a lot for me—more than he knows. He gave me a desire to believe in others, even when the desire for a friendship wasn't there at first; knowing him made me willing to reach out to prisoners that some might say had no hope of reform. I believe there comes a time when though there is no reason to hope, God calls us to hope for someone else—when we cannot see what He is doing within the heart of another person. For the first time in my life, I led someone to the Lord. Right in prison I had the overwhelming blessing of extending grace to a man who couldn't ever balance the scales of justice merely by doing time. None of us can do that. To be able to say, "Hey, Jesus paid your ransom. You are a free man, and sure you don't deserve it, but none of us do. Just take it, that's God's plan," was God's grace just flowing back at me. If I had not stayed those extra months, I would not have known how God can use a seemingly cruel delay as a way to bring about redemption.

Again, Jim

And then—again—there's Jim. As much as one would hope to never encounter their arresting officer repeatedly, it seems Jim and I haven't been able to get away from each other. After I served my sentence, I remember he came to hear me give my testimony at a Christian Businessman's Committee event. At first, I didn't see him; he stood outside, but within earshot of my voice. He came to see for himself, if my story was indeed the truth.

As I made my way up to the podium, I spotted Jim.

Aghast, I blurted with a tinge of paranoia, "What are you doing here? You have a warrant for my arrest?"

"No," Jim responded very matter-of-fact like. "I came to hear your testimony."

My initial fear of Jim's presence turned to honor as I turned around to announce to everyone, "Before I share my testimony, I want to introduce you to a man who saved my life. ..."

Jim later confessed, "I read about the event in the *Windsor Beacon* and I really came to see if you had legitimately changed. As a cynical cop, of course my first thought was, *Everyone gets saved in prison.* But then you shocked me as I heard your perspective, that prison indeed was the best thing that ever happened to you."

Jim became a believer two years before I did. We were born the same year. We also share this in common: our wives had a great impact on our faith. Shortly after my release, I called for his advice, to just help me stay clean and to have some accountability. Around that time, we knew God's hand had been orchestrating our relationship from the day we met, even before the day of the barricade.

"Gary, when I started walking down the lane in front of that farmhouse, I knew I had let my guard down with you—something we are instructed never to do. I'd been instructed to just kick the door down. The fact that I knew you also left me vulnerable, but though you had a violent reputation, we always made things work between us. And something told me this was the way I was to go with you."

"Yes. Jim, I'm certain you saved me from my own bullet. And for me being high on drugs to enter into some kind of ping-pong negotiation with you … all I can say is it was God." It's hard not to laugh when I think how I was convinced I had all the control—my gun, the drugs, calling the shots in how I planned to die. Hallelujah! A Sovereign God grabbed hold of that day and intervened despite what I wanted to do. I think it takes a great deal of misplaced faith to believe a man is in charge of his life. And quite a lot of arrogance to think someone's choices alone make or take a life. Jim and I both can speak to how God took over; we were players, but He was the orchestrator.

Like most people who are in law enforcement, seeing humanity at its worst can lead to bitterness toward the human race. Jim struggled too with this: "Before I became a Christian, I used to hate the criminal, but after I began to understand God's grace, I let go of that hate and realized I hated the *actions committed*—not people. That's when my attitude began to change toward people and my work. When I grabbed hold of that, I felt free to believe people can change, no matter what they've done."

Some days are marked as divine encounters with people. The day of the train accident, Jim appeared back in my life again at the hospital. His wife had a surgery scheduled and during her prep time, he learned about Kathy's death and that I had arrived in critical condition.

"Jim, why, why, did this happen?"

"Well, I don't know the answer, but I do know you'll be raising Brittany from a wheelchair. You are going to make it."

The truth is Jim didn't know if I'd be raising her, if

I'd even make it. But words are powerful. He was the last visitor I had that day, and God knew I needed to see the man who had saved my life before. Once again, his words had power over me. And then I fell into a coma.

Life without Kathy was a kind of suffering I wasn't prepared to face. God knew that and He provided the soul care I needed. Pastor Frank served as my shepherd and friend, feeding me God's Word to heal my wounds. Not only did He provide spiritually, but He also provided materially for my family. When Frank and Grace agreed to take Brittany in, they didn't consider how it might interrupt their lives; rather, with conviction, they took in my child as their own. They lived out what James 1:27 says to do, to look after the orphans and the widows in distress. Both Brittany and I qualified.

My story is full of such friends and encounters with God's agents, His people. He uses both friends and enemies to accomplish His purposes in our lives—both are a gift. And an enemy one day, can very easily end up being a friend in Christ the next ... when God is involved. I consider such relationships to be part of our reward in Ephesians 1:3, "All praise to God, the Father of our Lord Jesus Christ, who has blessed us with every spiritual blessing in the heavenly realms because we are united with Christ."

You never know how God is working out His plan. It continues to catch me by surprise.

CHAPTER 14

TESTING OF FAITH

*"Dear brothers and sisters, when troubles come your way,
consider it an opportunity for great joy. For you know that when
your faith is tested, your endurance has a chance to grow. So
let it grow, for when your endurance is fully developed, you will
be perfect and complete, needing nothing."*
— *James 1:2-4, NLT*

Surpised by Gratitude

No doubt we are all called to survive some test or
trial in life that has to do with God's purposes. I believe there are specific sufferings that each believer is
called to endure that correlate to their calling in life.
I don't at all mean to say that God made the train
crash into my truck; however, He allowed it—and I
was to endure it. After sharing my testimony, people
have often asked, "Aren't you mad at God for taking
Kathy?" It's a reasonable question.

146

Well, I know I went through the gamut of emotions anyone might expect to experience. But now one thing I am *not* is mad at God. First of all, it really does no good to be mad at God, and doesn't make a whole lot of sense if you believe He really is the only One you can trust to work everything out for good. My answer to those who ask is usually something like, "All I can gather is that God allowed Kathy to die—He saw everything. He knew when her last day on earth would be, and so I believe she fulfilled the purposes God had for her. Her assignment was over." I also take great comfort in knowing she is in the full presence of the Lord, where there is no suffering or pain.

Since the train accident, I continue to be grateful for all the obstacles the Lord has helped me through. Without them I'd have no reason to depend on Him, and I wouldn't know what He can do on my behalf. I think that is why James 1 says to "consider it pure joy as we face trials of many kinds." We can rejoice because sufferings make us stronger in our faith.

Trials can come on the most hopeful day or during the struggles of noonday; though the sun is out high, a storm can hit. Life's circumstances can change in a second, leaving you searching for one bit of blue sky. After the train accident, I figured my chances of another serious mishap had diminished according to statistics. But that wasn't the case.

On October 27, 2007 another testing of faith hit my family without warning. Thirteen years had passed by since the train accident—a lot had happened. In those years, I witnessed Brittany grow up into a strong, beautiful woman of God, like her mother. The years flew by raising Brittany, and during her high school years she really blossomed. We had great times together and I supported all of her rodeo events as a proud father, cheering her on and enjoying her love for horses. Upon graduating, Brittany decided she wanted to be a nurse. Her nurturing heart is something I admired as she tended to all my medical needs throughout all her school days. I knew she'd do well. College came quickly and I struggled to let her go, but I knew God was with her and His plan would continue to unfold. She met Ryan, and soon I had the blessing of escorting her down the aisle toward a God-fearing man, something a father prays for. I reflected on the seasons of change, as I drank my morning coffee. At peace. And grateful.

And then on October 27, 2007 a season of testing began. My son, Scotty, needed a ride to a new oil-drilling rig, south of Johnstown, so we headed out together toward County Road 19. A truck came out of nowhere straight at us—he moved into our lane and sideswiped the van. The left side-view mirror bashed through my window and shattered the glass. I felt the mirror strike my face and cut open my cheek. Wiping the blood off of my face, I watched the car race off in front of us, and I started to chase him, going as fast as my van would go, about 100 mph. I blazed on determined to get the license plate number, but his tires kept throwing up dust in front of me. Scotty called 911 and the highway patrolman told us to pull over so he could assume the chase.

"Sit where you are and don't move." And so, as hard as it was to submit to the officer's instructions, we waited. The officer boxed him in, where the man-on-the-run hit a bridge and totaled the pickup. The accident scene turned for the worse when it became a foot chase. A girl ran off, out of the truck, most likely because she was carrying drugs. During the chase, the officer's car rolled off a big embankment, leaving his back severely injured, so they had to airlift him to the hospital. I learned later the man who hit us had just been released on parole from prison. Already, this man had chosen a life on the run once again, which only led him back to the penitentiary.

Trying to take it all in, I wept before the Lord. "Lord, it feels like the enemy is trying to take my life. God, help me through this. Give me the strength to see this Your way." God answered that prayer and I began to feel gratitude flood over me, for all the times He had saved my life. He lifted me out of those fearful moments, and my heart cried out for this man who would end up back in prison. I knew my God could save Him too.

Thankfully, the accident only wrecked the van. Scotty and I were fine, though I know it drudged up some painful memories for both of us, thinking back to the train crash and what we lost that day. As the days passed on, the emotional impact of the accident faded and I felt more like myself, especially when the van came out of the shop with a fresh paint job. And then exactly thirty days later, another test came, the kind that makes you wonder if the enemy had been waiting for the right time to crush you.

The autumn air felt cleansing that morning as Scotty and I loaded up in my van around 10:30. Spotting the 55-mph speed limit sign, I noticed my speedometer needle at 45 mph as we headed toward County Road 17. As I approached the bridge, a car shot out over the incline toward us. I didn't see her coming. She crossed over the double-yellowed lines headed straight towards us. I had seconds to think, but there was nowhere to go on the bridge to avoid her. I froze. Upon impact, my van pushed backwards. Then, much like the train wreck, the rest is blurry when I try to recall it. The highway patrolman told me it was a 110-mph impact. Miraculously, both Scotty and I survived the head-on collision. In those short moments before I blacked out, something very wrong burned into my brain, how the woman came up over the bridge, before everything went dark.

Scotty and I were taken to the hospital. I don't remember much right after the accident but a trooper told me I kept asking for the whereabouts of my binoculars. It's strange to think that might have been my last request—must be the hunter's blood in me. I remember at one point calling our dear friends the Lightfoots. Shock had struck and I didn't even know what to tell them. Bursting out in tears I managed to say to Hannah, "just pray." The doctors once again swarmed around my room, letting me know what was broken: my legs, above and below my knees, my elbow, along with my collar bone, and six ribs. I had some internal injuries to battle—a bruised liver and a punctured lung. The doctors weren't thinking about surgery initially, but just trying to see if I'd pull through. Finally, I showed signs of my strength returning and surgery began. I remained hospitalized for two weeks.

Was this again a testing of my faith? I knew the enemy had followed me around enough to know where my scars were, and he usually hits where I'm most vulnerable. He isn't too original that way. Two accidents in thirty days felt beyond vicious. The only way to break free from the enemy's ridicule was to offer my praise to Him. So I focused on God and all He had brought me through.

I knew just thirty days ago, God had miraculously protected Scotty and me from harm's way. Then here we both were again, stunned by another brute-like accident. But alive. I remembered, too, that I could relate to this man who almost killed us. Drugs make you do things you'd never do on your own. God reminded me, "Forgive as I've forgiven you." Neither accident was a coincidence. And all three accidents were allowed by God. I prayed for strength to make the most of this opportunity so that He might be glorified. I appealed to 1 Peter 5:10 as a source of great truth: "So after you have suffered a little while, He will restore, support, and strengthen you, and He will place you on a firm foundation. All power to Him forever! Amen."

Scotty and I were both taken to rehab to recover from the car accident. It felt eerie being there with my son, as I reflected on the train accident. Yet we comforted each other, and I knew God performed a miracle once again. Thank God Scotty survived. He, too, underwent surgery. His femur bone shattered in eight different places, so the surgeon put in a steel rod. Together, we took it one day at a time.

The driver who hit us, Tammy, instantly died. I learned more about her story while in and out of surgeries. She had driven in from Florida to attend her ex-husband's funeral, staying in a hotel in Loveland. Tammy's life ended driving under the influence of drugs, impaired by cocaine. Senseless. Her son, sixteen, lost both parents within two weeks. And speculation did arise that the accident resulted from her own suicide mission. Scotty saw her bend over the dash to do a line of drugs before we crashed. She didn't have insurance, but the Lord took care of us and provided what we needed. My heart went out to that family. I know God wanted me to pray for Tammy's son, to empathize with the family. He gave me strength to do that, continually speaking to my spirit, "My grace is sufficient in your time of need."

The whole tragedy pushed me to reflect further on my foolishness years ago—how many times I drove my truck, high on cocaine. I remember a night when I got behind the wheel from Fort Collins to Windsor in a state of haughtiness. All of a sudden, I couldn't remember how I ended up there. I blacked out. I could have crashed or killed a child while on one of my reckless joy rides. I know my life also could have been snuffed out through the arrogance I felt when I was high—as though I were unstoppable. So many crimes are committed under the influence of drugs, as the conscience freezes up.

After about thirty days in rehab, Scotty went home; I wanted to go home too, but the doctors thought I should stay longer. Being overly determined, I insisted. Upon my release, emergency workers rushed me back in—my sugar levels had bottomed out. I remember the ambulance, strange voices, and bright lights with no other handle on what had happened to me. Again God sent a miracle my way.

"Brittany, your dad's sugar level sent him into a coma and when that happens, it usually results in permanent brain damage. ... And then just all the physical trauma. ... When your body starts shutting down, it is very hard to regain independence again. We are amazed!" God used this accident as a place to take hold of Him even more, to not withhold praise, to see His healing hands upon me. To survive two such critical accidents in a lifetime—for reasons God only knows—I'm certain He saved my life so I might complete my life's service and accomplish what He wants. Perhaps it's to share my testimony with a specific person I've yet to meet. Maybe it's to speak more blessings over my newest grandson, Bridger, to encourage him to grab hold of his calling earlier than Grandpa did; to grow up to advance the Kingdom of God, so he can fight against the false wisdom of this age.

Suffering isn't a popular thing to talk about—no one wants to hear about *that* promise. We are promised that "in this world we will have trouble" (John 16:33). But in addition to that assurance, we are also told His grace will be sufficient in every time of need (2 Corinthians 12:9). I didn't think I'd survive the county jail, let alone prison. My first reaction to suffering was to end my life. But by the grace of God, instead of death, He saved my soul and gave me eternal life. And just when I thought life might get easier, the train accident happened. Much like the three Hebrews—Shadrach, Meshach, and Abednego—at a time when I had surrendered my life more than ever before, the furnace blazed seven times hotter. Following the Way of Christ doesn't mean life is charmed or easy; rather it means we endure hardships, face persecution, weather spiritual storms, to find that He will never leave us or forsake us.

Sometimes, our trials come in long seasons. You

know the Israelites wandered in the wilderness for forty years, a journey which in reality was about an eleven-day trip. God doesn't allow such times of testing to prove how tough or weak are. Nor does he enjoy seeing us suffer. Sometimes we make the journey longer than necessary; sometimes we fall for the enemy's schemes. But I know when we submit ourselves to Him, God does indeed have the last say in the matter. When we actually rejoice in all circumstances, as Scripture commands us to, it is one of the most powerful ways we can glorify God.

God, Our Creator, knows what each of us can and cannot endure. Though some days seem impossible to live without Kathy, He takes me from strength to strength. There are days I want to curse my wheelchair and cry out to God to just clothe me in my heavenly body. But my God reminds me, *I know you best. I know what you need, and when you need it.*

We are told in Revelation that Satan has access to Heaven, and that part of the heavenly realm is where spiritual battles take place. Job 2 says:

> *On another day the angels came to present themselves before the LORD, and Satan also came with them to present himself before him. And the LORD said to Satan, "Where have you come*

from?"

Satan answered the LORD, "From roaming throughout the earth, going back and forth on it."

Then the LORD said to Satan, "Have you considered my servant Job? There is no one on earth like him; he is blameless and upright, a man who fears God and shuns evil. And he still maintains his integrity, though you incited me against him to ruin him without any reason."

"Skin for skin!" Satan replied. "A man will give all he has for his own life. But now stretch out your hand and strike his flesh and bones, and he will surely curse you to your face."

The LORD said to Satan, "Very well, then, he is in your hands; but you must spare his life."

God knew Job's devotion ran deep, that he would not curse Him and that Satan would not destroy his testimony. Jesus also knew Peter would deny Him three times, yet He would entrust him to build His church. In Luke 22:31-32 Jesus says to Peter:

"Simon, Simon, Satan has asked to sift all of you as wheat. But I have prayed for you, Simon, that your faith may not fail. And when you have turned back, strengthen your brothers."

I take great comfort in these passages, that all testing is allowed under the Lordship of God Almighty. Satan cannot do anything to us that God has not permitted. He is Sovereign over everything, even evil. And through the trial, the fire, He is forming us more into His likeness.

CHAPTER 15

THE HEALING

"But for you who fear my name, the Sun of Righteousness will rise with healing in his wings. And you will go free, leaping with joy like calves let out to pasture."
— Malachi 4:2

I believe in the healing power of God because He has healed me more times than I can count. In surviving innumerable surgeries and physical injuries His hand has been faithfully upon me, pumping breath into my lungs. As my struggles continue, no doubt I get tired of my banged up, overwrought body. Most days there is some physical concern to deal with, whether a foot wound festers or I'm fighting to keep my blood pressure down. And yet I want to proclaim to others, I am healed. Yes, I'm still in a wheelchair. Yes, I still rely on my doctors for advice and for medicine, but I'm keenly aware that God's sovereign hand is the One giving me life, and over and over He has saved me from death's door. Whether I'm chained inside prison doors or chained to my wheelchair, "the Word of God cannot be chained" (2 Timothy 2:9b). There is healing power through Jesus and His Word.

I've survived beyond the conventional wisdom of doctors. Through a heightened awareness of my human frailty, I don't hesitate to pray for a miracle. God's Word tells us that He is a God of signs and wonders: "God publicly endorsed Jesus the Nazarene by doing powerful miracles, wonders, and signs through Him, as you well know" (Acts 2:22). God performs miracles to show His power, to show authority over evil, and also meet the needs of His children. And you've read about some of mine. It is never a sin to pray for a miracle. He wants us to ask, to believe in Him *that* much. I believe He loves it when we ask for the impossible (Mark 9:23), because it shows our faith in what He alone can do— no one else. In my own need for healing on so many occasions, I've felt more conviction to pray for others in their afflictions and I believe that we've been too timid or doubtful to ask God for miracles, for healing. I find it interesting how exercising my faith for others in prayer has strengthened my own ability to pray for myself. He knows the healing touch each infirmity needs; and how easily we talk of how He healed the leper or the blind man, yet we hesitate to believe that He can heal us, too.

But what if the miracle doesn't come? Do we keep asking? Do we stop praying? I don't think we ever stop praying or believing that He can deliver us from all afflictions. But if deliverance doesn't come in the midst of our pain, I believe healing also can come through suffering, through a painful wound; and such a thought can be offensive when we see a loved one in pain, whether it is spiritual or physical pain. Yet I think about my own life: Through my suffering came my salvation and eternal life. I bear the scars of a man who went against everything God wanted for my life when I squandered His blessings and let drugs and money rule over me. Through my *choices* came the real suffering—shame, guilt, defeat. Those wounds turned to scars, marking my place of healing, and they are part of my story. No human ideology, no person, could take me from the pit I was in except for the saving work of Jesus Christ—My Healer. My dear friend Dick Gott would say, "there is a kind of suffering that heals." We don't like it, avoid it, and resist it with all our being. Yet God uses pain to draw us to Him, to take us to a place where He can mold us into His likeness. If we bear patiently in suffering, even if we have done nothing wrong, it pleases

God: "But if you suffer for doing good and endure it patiently, God is pleased with you" (1 Peter 2:20). Suffering produces humility in us, and when we are humble we allow God to take over.

Recently I had to deal with a serious wound on my foot. Because I don't have feeling in my legs, at first I didn't notice the bruise on the inside of my ankle, until it was somewhere between the size of a nickel and a quarter. I had read enough about foot wounds and paraplegia to know I needed the doctors to look at it. It didn't take long for it to spread and deepen, all around to the underside of my foot toward the outer side of my ankle bone. I'm not sure how many different doctors examined it each week when I'd go in for new bandaging. I kept hearing things like, "We've never seen anything like it," and "Don't count on this being completely healed." After a couple of months, the wound grew 178% bigger from when I first came in, and it soon blistered beyond the bandaging around my ankle. I'm not really sure how it happened, but something as minor as swinging my leg too hard up on the footrest of my wheelchair can cause such a serious lesion.

From week to week, more doctors continued to have a look. No one wanted to discourage me, but I knew amputation was a reality the doctors considered. After about three months of undressing and redressing my foot, there didn't seem to be any visible healing taking place, as the wound continued to deepen—exposing my heel bone. Continually I kept asking God to heal it and I knew He could do it in an instant. Medically speaking, I had every obstacle stacked against my healing. The diabetes, the scar tissue, my arteries, and seventeen years in a wheelchair made it all the more impossible for it to heal.

"Jan, how does it look down there?"

The nurse paused a long time looking down at the long ream of gauze. "Well, Gary, we're working on it." She didn't look me in the eye whenever I asked about it, so I knew hope for healing was diminishing. I had to leave it in God's hands and just keep praying. Paul charges us to do so: "Don't worry about anything; instead, pray about everything. Tell God what you need, and thank him for all He has done. Then you will experience God's peace, which exceeds anything we can understand. His peace will guard your hearts and minds as you live in Christ Jesus" (Philippians 4:6-7 NLT). As the weeks pushed on I just kept asking Him, kept giving thanks.

I continued to pray for healing, though there wasn't any physical evidence that my prayers were being answered. Discouragement began to fog around me and I couldn't shake it off alone. So one morning, I felt led to go see my friends at Herbies Auto Sales to pray over me. Lee Yoder has been a friend of mine through Christian Business Men's Connection (CBMC) and knows of my many physical struggles through the years. The folks at Herbies aren't your average car sales representatives: cars are secondary. The truth is God is doing some wild things at Herbies. Miracles are happening in the lives of employees as well as the casual customer who walks in the doors. My friend, Cindy, the general manager, took me over to one of the offices where many have received God's healing touch. That morning, Cindy brought in Melvin, an evangelist with one miraculous testimony. Born as a Hindu in a small rural town in South Africa under extreme poverty, Melvin understands what it means to overcome. He spoke about how the enemy uses discouragement to defeat us, keeping us from focusing on God, and how our Western minds forget the power of the spiritual realm. As we talked, their enthusiasm to pray over my foot increased and God's peace broke the oppressive discouragement I had been carrying. My own faith received a boost that day, and I knew more than ever God could heal it.

As I left Herbies praising God, He reminded me of His peace that passes all understanding, and I knew that even an amputated foot wouldn't keep me from the peace of God. I told Him, "Lord, I don't want to have another surgery ... I don't want to lose my foot; even though I don't use it, it *is* mine."

Not long after my encounter at Herbies, an unexpected turn for the better happened—the doctors couldn't believe it. The sore completely healed. Somehow the decayed tissue began to regenerate itself and my blood supply increased to foster healing. Each week the wound became smaller, and smaller, then down to the size of a quarter, then a nickel, then 100% healed. Praise God, He healed my foot! After seven months the wound completely healed. I give God the credit and know that even slower miracles are still miracles.

I believe His timing is always perfect, though when we have to endure a delay we are tempted to think prematurely, the answer is *no*, or that He is too late for us to see the breakthrough. I may not know how my wound impacted the nurses and doctors, who saw me about to lose my foot. And I know in those seven months, I stopped to pray with others who needed encouragement. If I had received a quicker healing, I know I wouldn't have had the opportunity to pray for the healing of those I ran into each week at the wound care center. I don't know if God chose to heal each person I prayed with, but I know He can do it. It's in such times, He burns away our self-centeredness; in such times, we more readily respond to His Word and what He wants us to do—to be content, giving thanks in all situations.

In this season of life I have a lot of time to pray and I'm so grateful for that. It gives me great joy to intercede for others. Circumstances in this life can change so quickly, for better or for worse. I've said prayers where God gives me His answer within less than a 24-hour period. And then some prayers I keep praying, even though I'm not aware of the fruit or I cannot see all He's doing. I have a choice every day, to let God use me or let my days be wasted in self-pity. I can't do everything I want to from a wheelchair. But I like to say, "I used to do 10,000 things. Now I can only do 9,000." It's not what happens to us; it's how we allow God to bring us through the adversity.

When I was on drugs, I had a mission. I knew what I had to do and no one stopped me for quite a while. But when I accepted Christ, my life mission totally changed. He took my life, a life bent on destruction, and saved me from the pit of hell.

I am a survivor of many circumstances from living in a fallen world, but so is every person. All of us in life are called to survive something. I survived the demise of my own sin because of the faithfulness of God. After the impact of the train, the medical team brought me back to life twice. I've survived paralysis, from the chest down. I also survived a head-on collision and close to twenty surgeries. As I reflect on all the mountains God has moved that were in front of me, my heart goes out to those who do not know God's help is there for *anyone* who calls on Him.

My prayer for everyone reading my story is to be encouraged what God can do—nothing is impossible with God. Keep believing, keep confessing to Him that you know He is working all things out for His glory in your life. Trust Him. He is moving in our lives, even when we do not see it (Romans 4:17). Perhaps you are reading this and made a commitment to Jesus Christ years ago and the fire of your faith has gone out. Do not doubt that, "He who began a good work in you will be faithful to complete it" (Philippians 1:6). Take a moment and ask God to fan the flame that the enemy is trying to snuff out.

Perhaps you are someone who doesn't know Jesus as Lord and Savior. Remember, you do not need to wait another moment to make a decision to follow Him. You may be like me; you have a trail of bad choices that are bogging you down. God gave us the ability to make choices, but our choices often lead us away from God, toward our passions and selfish desires. Romans 3:23 says, "For all have sinned and fall short of the glory of God." You may be someone who has tried to bridge the gap to God yourself through your own efforts. But no efforts can save us from our sin—we need Jesus. "For the wages of sin is death, but the gift of God is eternal life in Christ Jesus our Lord" (Romans 6:23).

If you know that you need Jesus to save you from your sin, I'd like to pray with you right now:

"Dear Lord, I thank you for this opportunity to pray with a soul in need of your salvation. I pray right now that the Holy Spirit would come and be evident to the person praying this prayer with me. Lord, make yourself real, wherever they are, just as You did for me in the prison cell, when Your light came into my world of darkness. Break the bondage of sin, so that Your cleansing power can free this soul in need of Your grace. We confess with our mouths that You are Lord and we repent from sin and turn toward You, Loving Savior: 'I believe that Jesus is the Christ, the Son of the Living God, and will receive Him as my Lord and Savior. We offer You our whole life and ask that You would show us how You want us to serve You. Today, God, connect my friend to other Christians so that this decision to follow You grows in a safe place, fertile soil, in the life of the Church. Strengthen them right now to not turn back, but to receive all the spiritual blessings You have for them. In the mighty and powerful name of Jesus. Amen!"

If you have just prayed this prayer with me, know that the angels are rejoicing with you right now! I encourage you to seek out a Bible-believing church and take steps toward a public confession among other Christians; and follow-up with learning about baptism under the guidance of a local pastor.

Scripture tells us that by His wounds we are healed. Sometimes we are in need of a spiritual healing. Sometimes it is physical or emotional. I'm certain God knows exactly what your need is right now. Nothing can separate us from God, not spiritual sickness or physical pain. I pray that my story has encouraged you to keep hoping, keep pressing into His healing power. Hold on to His Word: *A bruised reed He will not break, and a smoldering wick He will not put out.* Perhaps the weight of your burdens are so heavy that you are at a breaking point. Or maybe you feel so alone, your belief in Him is so fragile, that your faith has been smothered by the enemy's schemes against you. Maybe you are holding on to the bondage of unforgiveness and you haven't allowed God to heal your hurts. There are times we cry out, "God, I cannot take any more. I'm not even sure You are here." When we are in such a place, I believe that is when He tends to our souls so gently, as a loving Shepherd, Our Healer, binding up our wounds and carrying us to a safer place with Him.

Maybe you know of someone within your reach who is a bruised reed, an outcast in some circles, someone who believes they have failed one too many times; the pain of what they have done to loved ones runs too deep to even hope—the bruises don't heal. No one has ever told them about the healing balm of Jesus Christ. What bruised reed has God put in your path that you've tried to ignore? They are all around us. Some withered from sin. Some bruised from sickness. God calls us to restore one another, to hope, to have bold faith, and to believe God is big enough to change any life, even the heart of a hardened criminal. Who is He calling you to accept right now—exactly as they are?

When Jesus went to eat at the house of a Pharisee, a sinful woman came to meet him and poured out expensive perfume on His feet. The Pharisees' disdain for the woman clouded their ability to understand

God's forgiveness, so Jesus told this parable:

*When the Pharisee who had invited him saw this,
he said to himself, "If this man were a prophet,
he would know who is touching him and what
kind of woman she is—that she is a sinner."*
*40 Jesus answered him, "Simon, I have something
to tell you."*
"Tell me, teacher," he said.
*41 "Two people owed money to a certain money-
lender. One owed him five hundred denarii, and
the other fifty. 42 Neither of them had the money
to pay him back, so he forgave the debts of both.
Now which of them will love him more?"*
*43 Simon replied, "I suppose the one who had the
bigger debt forgiven."*
"You have judged correctly," Jesus said.
*44 Then he turned toward the woman and said
to Simon, "Do you see this woman? I came into
your house. You did not give me any water for
my feet, but she wet my feet with her tears and
wiped them with her hair. 45 You did not give me
a kiss, but this woman, from the time I entered,
has not stopped kissing my feet. 46 You did not
put oil on my head, but she has poured perfume
on my feet. 47 Therefore, I tell you, her many sins*

have been forgiven—as her great love has shown.
But whoever has been forgiven little loves little."
⁴⁸ *Then Jesus said to her, "Your sins are forgiven."*
—Luke 7:39-48

Jesus here is showing us how high, wide, deep, and broad His grace really is. And I am one who has been forgiven much. And because I have been forgiven much, I've got to tell my story, and let others know they, too, have been forgiven much. And that is where freedom abounds when we say to another, "Your sins are forgiven." And healing begins.

Yes, there still remains a healing for my earthly body, for my scarred legs and tired arms. How I long to be clothed in my resurrected body with no pain or suffering. But still, even in this worn-out flesh, I can loudly proclaim, "I'm healed! Through the power of Jesus Christ, yes, praise God, I am healed!"